D1282381

Photo by the Red Oak, IA, <u>Express</u>

# STORYTELLING TIPS

## How to Love, Learn, and Relate a Story

by
Duane Hutchinson

*To Mary*
*from Duane Hutchinson*
*June 23, 1988*

Foundation Books
P. O. Box 29229, Lincoln, NE 68529

Second Printing

Published by Foundation Books, P.O. Box 29229, Lincoln, Nebraska 68507.

# TABLE OF CONTENTS

# LIST OF PHOTOGRAPHS
of
Duane Hutchinson Telling Stories

**STORYTELLING TIPS,** from Duane Hutchinson

Dedicated
to the memory of my
grandmothers
Julia Harmon Hutchinson
and
Nettie Rowell Martin
who took time
to tell me
wonderful stories

Photo by Humberto Ramirez, Journal-Star Printing Co.

# Chapter 1

# STORYTELLING
## The Wine of Imagination

Each of us speaks in three languages, said a storyteller to me once. We speak in the language of the day (ordinary rational language), the language of the night (dreams) and the language of twilight (storytelling). Storytelling can have that wonderful, even mysterious, quality of entrancement.

The storytelling that I experienced as a child, from the adults who sat around the fire in the kitchen, or in the hayfield, or down at the country store, was a storytelling which gripped me--had a power that sneaked up on me. From casual talk back and forth there emerged one teller of a tale. We didn't know it was happening, sometimes, until he or she was well into the story. In fact, none of the group in those times would have called it storytelling--it was just talk. But, later, the word picture might haunt me. I realized I had been on a journey with that person. I had seen what the teller had seen and I had felt what the teller had felt. We had all tasted the wine of imagination.

There was an unwritten code among those in the group. Because it was unwritten it is difficult for me even today to say what the code was. But there were hidden lines of trespass. If a teller stepped across one of those invisible barriers, that teller paid a dear price--the price of being ridiculed by the group. If a teller became unbelievable in any but a humorous way, he got a sharp wisecrack from the nearest wit. "Y'er gittin' soft in the head, ain'tcha, Henry?" or, "You tipped a little too much of that jug." If he took on an air of importance because of the attention he was getting from the group, someone would "take him down a notch" by an interruption, or simply walking away to knock out a pipe, or another would innocently say, "I think the coffee pot's about empty."

Storytellers had to win their way into the group by making the first words count, having something worthwhile to say, sticking to the point, and shutting up when they were through. There was little forgiveness for an infraction of any of these rules.

When I started storytelling in the schools I knew that these rules were still in effect. Oh, children could be made to be quiet, to "be nice to the guest," but it would have been no fun to tell stories to an imprisoned audience. I knew I must be faithful to entice, or the listeners would "walk away" in their minds.

Here is one of my favorite stories, "Quito," by Freeman Tilden, which I've adapted from a book by John K. Terres called The Audubon Book of True Nature Stories. (New York: Thomas V. Crowell, 1950, 1958, pages 3-7). With the story I've made some side comments. If you wish, you can read the story straight through following only the boldface type.

**In the summer of 1956 a family of tourists was going through Olympic National Forest in Washington state when they saw the cutist little kitten come out of the forest.**

The story begins by showing a place and a "person"--the central character. Sometimes I've deliberately drawn out the beginning, describing the 100-foot tall Douglas firs, the Washington coastline etc., but I notice that the listeners don't show intense interest until that little character is introduced: **little kitten.**

**The father slammed on the brakes and stopped the car. The children jumped out of the backseat, ran around to the front of the car, picked the kitten up off the road, put it in the back seat with them and the family drove on.**

Immediately the central character has a problem and this is what grabs the listener (or the reader). Jesus began his parables by introducing a character with a problem: "A certain man went down from Jerusalem to Jericho and he fell among robbers who stripped him and beat him and departed leaving him half dead." That character had a problem, no question about it. "A certain man had two sons and the younger of them said, 'Give me...'" That character has a problem. The whole family has a problem in this story and it keeps the listener listening.

**The family had not gone far before the mother turned
around to see what kind of a kitten the children had picked
up..**

Mothers often like to know.  She's in character.

**..out in the national forest..**

Not the usual place to pick up kittens, so a subtle hint has been
dropped of trouble to come.

**..and she said, "Wait a minute! What kind of a kitten did you
pick up out there in the forest?" Because, even though it
mewed like a little house kitten, and it purred like a little
house kitten, it must have been this long** (hold hands apart to
suggest an enormous kitty) **and weighed ten to twelve pounds.
And furthermore it had a boney face.**

By now 98% of the audience knows there's trouble brewing and the
story leaves that to the imagination.

**So, the family took the kitten to the nearest forest
ranger station and asked what kind of a kitten the children
had picked up.**

Carefully note:  It wasn't the parents who had picked up the kitten,
it was the children.  Of course the parents had provided the opportunity and
the car etc. but the implication the parents seem to want to give now is, "The
kids did it.  You can never tell what kids will pick up, you know."

**Major Tomlinson said, "Well, what you've done is, you've
picked up a baby cougar--a mountain lion's cub.**

Here a specific name of a person is used for the first time.  It
gives that "I was there!" kind of quality--the storyteller even remembers his
name.  The man also has a military-like title giving him authority.  Cougar is
explained in case any listeners to the story didn't get it the first time.

**"You're fortunate you're all alive. If that mother moun-
tain lion had seen any one of you with her cub she might
have attacked you.**

"Any one of you" indicates that even the grownups might have been
"smackoed."  Things could have been worse than simply getting a scolding at the
Ranger Station!

**"You need to take that cub back to the exact spot where
you found it so that the mother can find it and feed it.
Otherwise, it will die."**

Here is a life-threatening situation for a baby kitten.  Both children and adults in an audience now care what is now going to happen.

"I'm not sure exactly where it was," the father said.  "Oh,
I know it was about twenty-five miles back down this road, but
all the forest looks the same."
"Then you might as well say that you've killed a little
baby cougar," said Major Tomlinson, "because it's going to die."

So, that's what happens when you interfere with nature.

The children began to cry.  "Please, Mr. Forest Ranger,"
they said, "isn't there something you can do?"

Forest rangers can fix anything.

"Well," said Major Tomlinson, "I have one idea.  I have
a couple of friends over in the next ranger station--Al and
Margaret Rose.  They're pretty good about raising wild animals.
They've had a pet badger, and a pet crow.  I'll call over and
see."

More specific names.  There's hope on the horizon.

Margaret answered the telephone.  "A cougar," she said.  "Do
you think we can raise a mountain lion?

Again we have the explanation that a cougar is also a mountain lion.
Her hesitancy to take on the task--she who has had more experience than anybody
around--is an indication of the enormity of the task.  She underlines the
hazard in the next line.

"Raising a coyote or an owl is one thing, but raising a
mountain lion is another.  Do you realize how big that cat will
get?"

I wondered myself how big a cat can get--haven't weighed a cougar
lately.

"A hundred and fifty pounds," said  Major Tomlinson.
"It'll be bigger than my husband," said Margaret.

This puts animal size in picture language with additional implica-
tions of danger.

"My idea," said Major Tomlinson, "is that you can raise
it for awhile.  Put it out every night so that it stays used
to the forest.  They're night creatures anyway.  And when it
gets strong enough to make it on its own you can leave it in
the forest."

We're getting additional information about the cougar, and some indication that Major Tomlinson is a senior forest ranger over the Roses.

**"Well,..."**

Margaret still hesitates.

**"...bring it over," said Margaret, "and we'll try."**
**So Major Tomlinson took the little cougar over and put it down on Margaret's kitchen floor. It slipped and slid on the slick linoleum.**

Here the children laugh because they can see the stumbling kitten trying out a slick floor for the first time.

**Then on the rug it walked along so precisely that Margaret said, "My! You're a regular little princess, aren't you!**

Here we have the first indication that the kitten is a female. This has been an unasked question in many of the children's minds, but they've had to wait because Quito has been an "it" so far.

**"I'm going to call you Quito, a Spanish word for princess.**
**"Quito, you're hungry. That's why you're scratching at the stove and the refrigerator.**

Here we get a picture to form in the mind--a kitten reaching up and scratching on the refrigerator and stove. The picture comes from a fragment of a woman's dialogue, but the listener does the creation.

**"And I don't have any fresh cougar milk for you.**

Not even any day-old cougar milk. It's a private little joke between a kindly forest ranger's wife and a wild creature. It is also a foreshadowing of trouble to come.

**"But I do have some cow's milk."**
**Margaret got out a carton of Meadow Gold milk and poured it into a pan on the stove to heat. She got out the baby bottles and nipples from when their boys were little.**

Cow's milk is a poor substitute as we shall soon see. I use a particular brand name for the milk so the story will be more specific and believable.

If you were writing this story you probably would avoid saying "got out" twice in a row, but this is a told story with the emphasis on the content--milk and bottles--not on literary style. Anyway, it is an active style in which parallel phrases often give valuable emphasis.

**Margaret was just testing a warm bottle on her wrist  when
Al walked in the door.**

This sentence is a transition. We didn't have to wait for the milk
to heat and tediously watch the bottles being filled and the nipples screwed
on. No, that is all assumed. Watch these transitions in the story.

**"Margaret!" Al said. "Where did you get that cougar?
Where did you get that mountain lion?"**

Al is no dummy. He's a forest ranger and he knows about cougars (see
also the repetition for cougar-equals-mountain lion) and he knows they're
nothing to mess with. Here I emphasize once more the danger of this exotic
animal and make use of <u>another</u> person's testimony. Someone <u>other</u> than the
storyteller /writer must <u>show what</u> you want to show in order to <u>make</u> it believable! The narrator is there to show and introduce characters and scenes but
not to give opinions.

**"Some tourists picked it up on the road," Margaret said.
"Well, what are <u>we</u> going to do with it?" Al said.**

A purist would probably want to say, **"Al ASKED."** But can't the
storyteller be forgiven for rushing along, like Ernest Hemingway, saying, "He
said," and, "She said," recognizing that these are simply tools to forward the
main enterprise? Certainly the storyteller who said, "He groaned," and,
"She breathed," or, "He ejaculated," would be laughed out of court! Just try
that last one once with any high school group and see what happens!

**"Raise it?"
"We can't raise that cougar. Why, it'll be bigger than I
am some day...and twice as dangerous."**

Now, this little joke is lost on all but adults. But women who have
had to put up with any unbearable macho-types may get a chuckle out of this. A
novelist would have to add something like, "and," he added with a sly grin,
"twice as dangerous." It is one of the luxuries of the storyteller that the
teller can leave out many tiresome explanations because the facial expressions,
hands and other body language do what is needed.

All of this brings to mind why it is important that the storyteller
learn to reformulate the story in his own words--to recelebrate the story and
let listeners share in the act of re-creation of the story on the spot.  I
winced a little when I wrote, **"It'll be bigger than I am some day."** The writer
in me wanted to say, **"It will be bigger than I am some day,"** but  no forest
ranger would talk like that unless he had lace on his pants. He'd probably
say, **"It'll be bigger'n I am."** In other words, don't be afraid to use contrac-
tions. Follow Rudolf Flesch in this. We have one language for oral language
and another for written. We are talking about oral language now.

**"Major Tomlinson said that if we'd put the little cougar
outside every night it would stay used to the forest and when**

it is strong enough it can make it on its own."
    "Well," Al said, "I suppose if Major Tomlinson wants us to
try, we can try."

If the boss wants us to do it we'd better do it, even if he's wrong. Do you see how all this is leading to an impression of trouble coming? Here are strong, seasoned forest rangers who are going against their better judgment to raise a dangerous mountain lion.

Al reached over and picked up little Quito by the back of
the neck, the way a mother kitten picks up its babies by the
loose skin at the back of the neck.

Small children enjoy nodding their assent because they all seem to know that mother cats pick up their kittens that way and want you to know they know.

We also have a silent, swift, confirmation that Al has made his decision. He has taken the first step on a hazardous journey. He has also willingly accepted the name "Quito."

Al said, "That little mountain lion was a growling,
scratching, biting little bunch of fur. She raked me across
the back of the hand and then tried to lick the blood off the
back of my hand—getting entirely the wrong idea."

Here we have Al as the narrator for a moment. It seems to work. Again, our imaginations are allowed to fill in the scene of the struggling man and kitten. And Al's ominous comment about getting entirely the wrong idea (about whose blood to drink) is not missed by young audiences. The tension builds.

Al managed to get his fingers into Quito's mouth and
forced her jaws open,

(Storyteller acts it out.)

stuffed in the bottle of milk and..(pause)she chewed the
nipple right off the bottle.

Children, and sometimes adults, laugh at this.

Al got another nipple, screwed it on

(Storyteller acts it out.)

and stuffed it in. (pause) She ripped that one open!

More laughter.

**Al said, "Quito!   How can I feed you if you're going to chew up my tools?"**

I learned the hard way to be careful about my language at this point. One time I was at a strict, private girls' school, soon after I had learned this story.  I made the mistake of saying to those teenagers, "Quito! How can I feed you if you're going to chew up my nipples." It was quite awhile before we got the classroom back to order again.

The direct quoting of dialogue seems to be valuable though, and I use it wherever I can.  It's fun to try classical stories, such as fairy tales, entirely of dialogue--making it up on the spot.

**Al got the third nipple and screwed it on. Quito was getting the idea by this time and did a little more sucking than chewing. She drained the whole bottle. Then she wanted more of that stuff.**
**Al said, "She kept us up most of the night--wanting more of that stuff.**

I realize this is anthropomorphism.  It's almost as if we are quoting Quito's enthusiastic, if vulgar, request for "stuff."

**"The next morning we were running out of milk**

This is a powerful technique:  Showing what happened by the <u>results,</u> the <u>effects</u> rather than having the narrator <u>tell</u> that Quito drank a lot.

**"and Quito was swelled up like a pup."**
**But during the day Quito got sick--Oh! So sick!**

The children knew it.  They saw it coming and they identify with Quito.

**By nightfall her little abdomen was swelled up like a balloon and Al and Margaret were fairly sure they were going to have a dead cougar on their hands in a few hours.**
**But, Al and Margaret Rose were shrewd about animals. They concluded that she was sick on that cow's milk.  If it had only been  mother's milk with the right enzymes and all it would have been all right.  But that homogenized, pasteurized cow's  milk had probably not only made Quito sick to her stomach but constipated as well.  So, they decided to give her an enema.**
**They  got some warm water and a rubber bulb syringe and Al said, "Trying  to give her that enema was like fighting a  buzz saw and threading a needle at the same time."**

Listeners at this point often laugh with a relief of tension.  Al's metaphorical way of describing the struggle avoids poor taste and yet conveys a moving (pardon the pun) picture!

Al said, "I followed her outside with a flashlight until I was reasonably sure she was all right then put her back in her box. We wondered whether we would have a dead cougar on our hands the next morning.

"But the next morning there was no question whether she was alive or dead. Quito was making enough racket we could hear her all the way to the other end of the house.

"Margaret came out and found Quito leaping up the side of her box and chewing on the wood of the box. Margaret said, 'All right Quito, no more cow's milk for you. You're going to eat whatever we eat from the kitchen table.'"

Al and Margaret Rose also knew that many wild animals will chew up adult food, swallow it, get it partially digested and then regurgitate it and give that to their little ones.

At this point children divide along age lines. Fourth graders and up usually wrinkle up their noses and show distaste at the thought of animals providing regurgitated food.

Al said, "We were pretty good at chewing and swallowing and, I guess, digesting, but we weren't very good at throwing up on command whenever Quito wanted to eat.

At this the realization of what is being said is picked up by some third graders and many children will say, "Yuk!" or some such expression.

"So, I took some well-cooked steak and chewed and chewed that in my mouth until I felt it was partly digested. Then I took that out, gave it to her and she liked that.

"Yuk."

"Then I mashed up some garden peas with a fork and she liked that. And it got so she would eat whatever we ate from the table. Mashed potatoes? Oh, that was good, especially if it had gravy on it.

"Yum."

"One day she even ate some creamed spinach.

"Oh! Yukkk!!!"

"But her favorite thing--seventh heaven--was canned sardines.

"Oh, Yukkk!!! Gross!"

"Whenever we'd twist open a can of sardines, she'd come leaping from wherever she was in the house and try to climb the table  leg to get to those sardines.  She could smell the fishy smell.

"So,  I'd scrape out the can into her pan and try to set the pan down on the floor without losing a hand in the process. She was  getting  so  big and strong by this time that  I  was half afraid of her.

"She  was, in fact, so strong that she could pick  up  her whole pan in her teeth and carry it all around the room, spill- ing sardines wherever she went.

"I had to get a hammer and some nails and nail her pan down to  a board in the floor to keep her from carrying sardines all around the room.

(Laughter.)  I don't know if it's the fun of pounding nails into the kitchen floor or simply the picture of the mountain lion carrying the pan, but the children generally laugh at this point.

"She was getting long and beautiful.  When she'd walk through a doorway her back would flow and ripple.  We wished we would have weighed her when we first got her, but we didn't think  of it until one day when we put her on the bathroom scale.  She weighed fourteen pounds!

A few little first grade boys will generally give out with a loud, "Geeee!"

"We weighed  her a few days later and she weighed  nineteen pounds!

"Geee!"  A few more boys join in and now a few girls.

"We  weighed  her a week later and she  weighed  twenty- nine pounds.

Now comes a whole chorus of, "Geeee!"

At this point one of the macho boys will sometimes interrupt the group and say, "That's not as much as I weigh."

"She was literally growing by leaps and bounds.
"She  wanted to sleep in the house, but we weren't sure  we wanted  a hundred and fifty-pound mountain lion  roaming  around the house at night.

Repetition of the weight outlook and of the mountain lion being a night creature.

"So, we'd put her out the back screen door every night. But, she'd  be so disappointed in us. 'Put me out the door at night? Night's the cuddly time,  night's the time to crawl up in the lap to be held and petted and played with.'

The children often scrunch up and hug themselves. They know what it feels like to be held and cuddled and played with at night.

> **"She'd crawl up the back screen door and hang by her claws hooked through the screen and cry and watch us in the kitchen.**

Yeah. Our cat does that.

> **"So we'd go off in the back bedroom and try to get some sleep, but do you think we could get any sleep?**

Children of the third grade and under will chorus in response to this rhetorical question: "Noooo!" From fourth grade up they're too sophisticated to answer.

> **"No, she'd come around the side of the house, jump up on the bedroom screen and cry and watch us in bed and wonder why she couldn't come and get in bed with us.**

Chuckles.

> **"One night," Al said, "after about two hours of that Quito serenade, with her hanging on the window crying, I looked up at her..** (yawn)

I half yawn when I say it and many of the smaller children will yawn with me.

> **"..and said, 'Quito, are you going to keep me up all night with that crying? I guess if you're going to keep me up all night anyway you might as well be in the house. But** (shaking my finger sternly) **you're going to have to be toilet-trained if you're in the house...**

Nervous laughter from the children. Some nod up and down in exaggerated agreement. "Yes, that's what you have be is toilet-trained."

> **"'..and how are you going to toilet-train a thirty-going-on-forty-pound cougar?'**

I have to hurry at this point and go on with the story or I'll get lots of shrill advice about toilet training. I've been told to spank the kitten, make it sit on the stool, push its nose in its messes, etc. etc. But I quickly add:

> **"Margaret and I found out a way that works and it will work for your puppy or kitten. We simply put Quito in the kitchen for five nights in a row. We put newspapers all over the whole kitchen floor so it didn't matter where she went. Each morning we picked up any newspapers she hadn't**

bothered until, by the end of five nights she was down to one
newspaper.

"She was so careful after that,  she would always go to
her newspaper.  We substituted  a box of sand after while  so
she could cover everything up the way cats like to do.

"She was well trained all right,  but sort of toilet
trained in reverse.  Whenever  she  was  out  in  the  woods
somewhere, playing, and had to go, she'd come running back to
the house and scratch on the door to get in to her box of sand.

This generally always brings laughter.  People can see the kitten
insisting on getting back into the house.

"The sand out in the woods wasn't good enough for her.

"We decided,"Al said,"that if she were that well trained
she could  sleep  in  the  house.   But  we had a  little
difference  of opinion  with her about where.  We had thought
that  she  could sleep in the kitchen.  She thought she ought
to be able to sleep in the bedroom!

(Laughter from the children.)

"And  she had very precise ideas about where she thought
she ought to be able to sleep....

The children interrupt at this point with extravagant nods and even
make motions to show that they know pets like to sleep on the bed.

"...right on top of the bed...

(Laughter)

"...between Al and Margaret."

(More laughter and nods of agreement.)

Al said, "No way was I going to have a  one-hundred  and-
fifty-pound  mountain  lion sleeping between Margaret and me
in bed some day. I would make her lie down on the hooked rug at
the foot of the bed, which she would do.  She would curl up and
put her tail over her nose to keep her nose warm during the
night.

More laughter and nods of assent.    Apparently this sleep character-
istic is also familiar to children because they chuckle and enjoy sharing in
common knowledge.

"But many a night I would wake up at two or three o'clock
in the morning and feel something warm and furry against my
cheek.

Children laugh.

**"And it wasn't Margaret.**

Teachers and high schoolers laugh.

"Quito had come sneaking over the foot of the bed so cautiously that I hadn't even heard her come. But by that time I would be so sleepy that I wouldn't even go to the trouble to put her down on the rug again. She would sleep with us the rest of the night."

Quito loved Al. Nothing she loved more than to crawl up into his chair with him or into bed with him and rub her cheek against his cheek.

She didn't love neighbor men too well and they were afraid of her. When they came into the yard with their U. S. Forestry pickups, they'd sit in the yard and honk the horn until someone would come and rescue them. They knew that Quito's favorite place to sleep during the middle of the day was out on a tree limb that hung over the yard.

Al said, "When we'd let Quito out in the morning she'd run up her tree, crawl out on a limb, drop down on her belly and let her legs hang down and watch for something interesting to come by underneath, such as a rabbit...

Groans of anticipation.

"...or squirrel..

More groans.

"...or chicken.

"Gross!"

"She'd stick her chin out in the sunshine and warm her face and act like she was asleep. But she was no way asleep.

"As soon as something moved down below her, her tail would begin to flick."

I'll make motions with my hand to imitate the motion of a cat's tail when it senses prey.

Al said, "We used to have quite a few chickens, but we didn't have many chickens any more. We had lots of bloody feathers blowing around the yard, but not many chickens.

Choruses of, "Gross!"

We are communicating  a lot without saying it.  The storyteller is not only allowing the listeners' imaginations to draw conclusions about something too "awful" to mention (thus making it more powerful than if it were told outright) but is laying the groundwork for--foreshadowing--trouble to come.

> "One  day," Al said, "Margaret and I were standing in  the kitchen looking out the window to where Quito's tree was.  Here came a happy little rabbit, hopping across the yard.
> "Quito's tail began to flick.
> "I simply got my watch out and thought I'd measure how long it would take to transform a happy,  healthy rabbit into  little bits of bloody fur blowing across the yard.

I act out looking out the window to see the action and looking down at my watch to time the action.

> "Three and one-half seconds!"

"Ohhh, yukkkk!"  Groans of misery and delight.

The children have <u>seen</u> what happened without having it spelled out to them (which would have weakened the effect).

There are flurries of little side comments among the children as they get settled down again.

> Al said, "We knew we were in trouble.  Some of the little games Quito used to like to play as a kitten weren't nearly so funny any more.
> "One  was  a  little game called 'Grab' or 'Snatch.'  If anyone happened to be sitting on the sofa with a hat or glove in the lap, Quito would s-n-e-a-k up behind the piano and watch for her big chance.
> "'Aaaaahhgh!'

I scream and leap toward the listeners.  The children jump violently, then laugh and giggle at each other.

> "She'd make a flying leap,  grab the hat and run down  the hall, chewing on the hat.  We didn't dare go down and try  to take the hat away from her.  Oh, no.  She'd get your hand.  The only safe way was to take a throw rug and throw it all over her until she was in the dark and couldn't tell where the 'enemy' was.

This identifies it as a game.  Children rub their hands with glee.

> "We'd  pull back the edges of the rug until a corner of the hat would appear, then grab the hat and pull.

I act out the pulling up.

"She'd come right up with the hat.

Teeth bared, I play Quito's role.

"We'd twist her up. Like twisting up a child in a swing we'd spin her around until she'd get dizzy.

I cross my eyes and act dizzy. Children laugh.

Then she'd drop the hat, go over, crawl up in Al's lap and want to be petted...

Children cuddle and act out being petted.

...and get her head straightened out.

Laughter.

One day a neighbor lady came over to visit--a neighbor who lived twenty-eight miles away, over in another forest range, and didn't know about Quito.

Children put their hands to their mouths in horror. Many will say, "Oh!  Oh!"

She drove into the yard, got out, adjusted her hat and coat and started for the house.

More cluckings and, "Oh! Oh's," from audience.

She made  it to the house because Quito wasn't in her tree.
Margaret  came to the door and was so happy to see a neighbor  lady  she didn't even think about Quito. She invited the neighbor in. They walked through the dining room and into the living room,  sat down on the sofa and talked about the art work around the wall.

All this time the children's hands are over their mouths, ready to muffle a scream.

After  awhile Margaret thought she'd go out to the  kitchen to fix hot water for tea. While Margaret was gone the neighbor lady saw her opportunity to pull off her hat and laid her hat in her lap.

Now and then a child will burst out with: "Don't do it!" and then look around sheepishly, realizing that he has spoken out of the audience.

The neighbor looked around, trying to be so polite.

I imitate sitting primly, smiling sweetly, and looking around innocently.

**Quito crawled up behind the piano, watched the hat from
between the pictures on the piano, and leaped across the living
room...**

By this time the children are ready, prepared not to be surprised a
second time. I act out the leap in slow motion doing a throaty, but soft, cry.

**...grabbed the hat and ran down the hall with it.
The poor neighbor lady was about to barf over the side of
the sofa.**

Imitate act of throwing up over the side of the sofa. The children
simply go into fits of laughter at this one.

**Margaret said, "I chased Quito down the hall, got the rug
over her, pulled up the hat, twisted her until she got dizzy
and let go.
"I took the hat back to the neighbor. It wasn't very
pretty any more. It was sort of wet and bedraggled and the
feather was gone.
"The neighbor said,** (imitating person on the edge of nau-
sea) **'I think I'm going home. I don't feel very good.'
"And we weren't feeling very good either,"** Margaret said.
**"We knew we were going to have to do something about Quito. Al
was soon to be transferred to a new ranger station where he
would be training other people. We didn't dare take Quito with
us; it was too dangerous.
"We called everybody we could think of and asked if they
wouldn't like a free kitten.**

Apparently most of them have been through this because they show a
lot of emotion--humor, dismay, sadness.

**"Some people were interested until they found out that our
'kitten' weighed forty-three pounds.**

Laughter.

**"Then they said, 'You'd better take her to a zoo.'
"Well, we didn't want to take her to a cold impersonal
zoo!**

Here is the first of what will be repeated several times, like the
tolling of a bell, the foreshadowing of the sadness to come.

"So, we put it off. But one day a man came through the country with a dairy truck.

Immediately alert children will start the clucking and the, "Oh! Oh's."

"Why he thought he could start a dairy route out in the middle of Olympia National Forest, I don't know.

A needed reminder of the geography and remoteness that made such a raising of an exotic animal possible.

"He stopped his van in the yard. Got out. Walked around to the back...

Here we're using a device we've used before and will use again: a deliberate slowing down of the action as the prelude to a catastrophic event. Tension increases.

"...opened up the back van doors, set out two trays, two bottles of milk, a bottle of cream, a pat of butter, and a dozen eggs. He was going to make a sales pitch to Margaret. He slammed the van doors and started toward the house with those two trays of tinkling bottles...

The implication is that if Quito wasn't awake before she surely will be now with all those sounds.

"..and started for the house.
"Well, he didn't make it to the house. He made it as far as Quito's tree. Quito leaped out of the tree with a terrible cry. The man jumped aside and she just missed him. The poor man left a trail of broken bottles all the way back to that van. He jumped into the van, slammed the door, looked over the edge of the glass and said, 'Get that mountain lion out of here!'
"And we realized that was exactly what we were going to have to do. So, we called the Seattle zoo.
"The Woodland Park Zoo people called us back in about an hour and said, 'Yes, we have an empty cage and we would like to have a cougar in our exhibit.'

The word "exhibit" is not lost on many children. They realize there is something awful about 'being exhibited.'

"'But, you need to understand that an animal you've raised in your home, that's slept in your bedroom and eaten from the kitchen table, may not make the adjustment living in an iron cage in an impersonal zoo.

Here too is a foreshadowing phrase that will become a repeated, echoing symbol.

"So, we put it off a little longer until one day Al had another close call. He had to go into town to get some sup- plies. He jumped in the car and he said later he didn't even think about Quito. She used to ride in the car when she was a little kitten. She'd jump up in the back seat and ride right under the back window. But that day he didn't think of her.

At this point a tragic look comes into the faces of the children. I have found out that they believe Quito is going to get run over. Many of them have had pets run over by cars.

"He drove into town, forty-two-miles, looked up into the rear view mirror to make a left-hand turn and there was Quito, grinning,

Children chuckle in glee (and relief) at seeing her up to a trick on an adult.

" ...up in the back window. She had been very quiet because she knew she wasn't supposed to be there."
Al said, "I shook my finger at that rear view mirror and said, 'Quito! You mustn't be in town! But I'm not going to drive forty-two miles back out into the country with you ei- ther. You're going to have to stay in a locked car.'"
Al said he parked his car way off at the corner of the parking lot and hoped no one would even see Quito. He rolled each window down about so far...

Make space with finger for three inches.

...so she could get fresh air but wouldn't be able to get a paw out and hurt anybody...

I always hope that this last sentence may save some little dog from suffocation by a member of the audience who follows Al's example.

...locked each door, he thought, quite securely and went into the store. But it took him longer to get through check-out line than he had expected. By the time he got back out into the parking lot he said that his car was completely surroun- ded—he couldn't even see his car for people.
Al said, "By the time I got to the edge of the crowd I was sure that somebody had been destroyed—was bleeding to death on the sidewalk and everybody was standing around wondering how that happened.
"A man on the edge of the crowd saw my ranger uniform and grabbed my sleeve. He hung right on—wouldn't let me go.

"'Ranger!  Ranger!' he said, 'You gotta do something quick.
There's a mountain lion in that car there.'
   "'Oh Good!' I said, 'She's in the car then.'
   "'Yeah, she's in THE CAR.'
   "'That's where I want her.  She sleeps in the bedroom  at
home.'
   "'She what?'"

   And at this point I imitate a little man looking up at the taller
ranger.  When he hears about the bedroom he swings around and as he says, "She
what?" he looks Al up and down as if to try to figure out this strange being.
It always brings a laugh.

   Al said, "I went through the crowd—'Excuse me. Excuse me.'

   Imitating with my body squeezing through a tightly packed crowd.

   "I got out my keys and as I was bending down trying to  get
the car door open I could hear the sound of running feet.

   People start to laugh, already anticipating what is happening.

   "People were taking off across that parking lot. They
weren't going to stay around if I was dumb enough to open up
that car door.

   All this, of course, is a way of reinforcing the image in the listeners' minds of what a large and dangerous-appearing animal Al has.  Again, much
stronger than saying, "He had a great big cat in his car—really enormous etc."
   "When I got the door open Quito leaped up, put one paw on
each  shoulder and started licking me in the face with that
old saw-tooth tongue of hers.

   I act out being licked in the face and trying to protect myself with
grimaces and pushes against an imaginary beast.

   "I said, 'Quito!  Get down in the back seat.  You are so
rough.'"

   Now Al is just another pet owner trying to keep his pet in line.  So,
we are trying to keep the listener identified with Al but still remind that
same listener of what a strange creature he's dealing with.

   Al got in, slammed the door, and started for home.  "But,"
Al said, "All the way home Quito rode with her back feet on
the back seat and front feet on my shoulders and watched the
cars go past outside the window.

   I act out Quito's antics,  following passing cars with slow-turning
head motion and children laugh to imagine the surprise other people get when
they see her.

"People would swing around and stare! (laughter) As if they couldn't believe what they were seeing.

"That night," Al said, "Margaret and I talked until almost midnight about what to do. What to do?

"By the next morning we knew what we had to do. We got up early and put Quito in the back seat of the car.

"Margaret said, 'Shall we put in her little harness?'

"I said, 'You might as well. We won't need it any more.'

"By the time we reached Seattle," Al said, "and drove into the zoo, Margaret was crying and I had such a big lump in my throat that I could hardly swallow. I felt like I was taking a member of my own family to prison.

You see, women cry and men only get lumps in their throats--and ulcers, and heart attacks.

Up to this time we haven't stated that Quito is being given up and committed to the zoo, but it isn't necessary--better to <u>show</u> what's happening by showing the effects on other people.

"Quito was happy, looking around as if to say, 'What new game is this we're going to play today?'

There is something terrible about her sweet innocence, her trusting spirit.

"I took her out on her short leash and every animal in that zoo let out a trumpet or a shriek to let us know that they knew another animal was coming into the zoo.

"Quito ran into her cage and investigated every corner. She seemed happy until the cage door clicked shut and we weren't in there with her. She suddenly looked frightened, put her paws up on the side of the cage as if to say, 'You can't do this to me. You can't go away and leave me like this.'

"Margaret said, 'Hurry up. Let's get out of here. If we can't take her with us, <u>Let's go!</u>'

"As we left Quito began to cry--a terrible, mournful, almost human cry that we had never heard her cry before. She hung up on the side of the cage and reached through the bars to try to touch us.

"We almost ran across that parking lot to our car and drove away. I promised myself that I would come back to see her as soon as possible.

"But, I was so busy it was almost a week before I returned. When I was within two blocks of the zoo, I suddenly heard Quito cry. It wasn't that terrible, mournful cry; it was a happy, welcoming cry that I used to hear when I'd come back to the ranger station.

"I ran to her cage. She hung up on the bars, reaching toward me and I said, 'Quito, I'll go find a key and get in with you.'

"I came up to the zoo keeper and said, 'I want a key to the cougar cage. I want to get in and see my pet, Quito.'

"He looked at me and said, 'Oh, no you don't. Not in that cougar cage. That's the most dangerous animal we've got in this zoo.'

"'Oh, surely not,' I said. 'She sleeps in our bedroom at home and we feed her from the kitchen table.'

"'Well-l-l, we don't feed her from the kitchen table. She almost got one of the men. When we feed her we push raw meat under the bars with a long stick. When we clean her cage we stand back with a high-pressure hose.'

"'Awww,' Al said, 'You don't need to treat her that way. She's a nice kitten. Get in and make friends with her.'

"'Well, you can go make friends with her if you want to.' He handed me the keys. 'But don't say I didn't warn you, Ranger.'"

This interchange is a way of showing the problem of "domesticating" exotic animals and causing them to lose their fear of human beings. The zoo keeper sees her as a stranger and particularly dangerous without the shyness of forest creatures. There is peril in familiarity!

A little girl was recently mangled and disfigured by a "pet" cougar that wandered over from the neighbors. It is against the law in Iowa to keep exotic animals without a license.

Al said, "As I opened her cage door I wondered if I was making a terrible mistake. Quito reached around the edges of the bars with more claw sticking out than I had ever seen before.

"As I entered, the cage door clicked shut behind me and Quito leaped up on my shoulders, hung onto my neck, digging in deeper than I preferred.

"I said, 'Quito! Get down! You're so rough.'

Here is an echo of the command that Al had given out in the store parking lot. In this case it is much more serious and children show their awareness of the hazard by watching me with big round eyes and holding their hands over open mouths. Al reaches a new understanding with Quito after his absence.

"I managed to find an overturned bucket in the cage and sat down on it. Quito leaped up on my lap, but she was so big by this time that she hung over on both sides all the way to the floor.

Children usually laugh at this, partly as a release of tension, but also at the picture of this huge animal clambering over a man's lap.

"I rubbed her little round ears and stroked her back.

The long sweeping motions of this "stroking" indicate again how huge this mountain lion had grown.

"She would reach up and sandpaper my face with her rough tongue. I'd push my fist in her mouth, something she enjoyed, and pull the little tuft of hair under her chin.

Reminders of her size...and rough affection.

"But, after an hour," Al said, "wrestling her on my lap, I was just simply worn out. Every time I tried to stand up, or get into a different position, she'd jump up and try to hang on the back of my neck.
"At last I said, 'Quito, I've got to go home. I can't stay here all night.'
"As I made for the door she ran ahead of me and looked up as if to say, 'Well, take me home.'
"I said, 'Quito, I can't take you home. It's too danger-ous.'
"Then she threw her shoulder against the door and wouldn't let me out.
"I said, 'Quito! Now let me out! I've got to go home.'

At this point I see panic in the faces of some children and uncon-trollable tears are starting in others. Children have been reminded of E. T. as he pointed his finger at the starry sky and said, "Home! Home!"

"I had to edge my way sideways out that door. When the door clicked shut, Quito began to cry—that same terrible cry I'd heard when I left the first time. I ran to my car, turned around and said, 'Quito, I'll come back to see you just as soon as I can.'
"But, I became so busy setting up that new forest ranger station that it was three weeks before I could come back.

To small children (as to Quito) three weeks is an interminable age. They've waited for their daddies to come home from long business trips.

"When I came within two blocks of the zoo I listened for Quito's cry, but I didn't hear it. I ran to her cage and found it empty, the door standing open. I ran to the zoo keeper. 'Where's Quito?' I asked. 'Where's my pet cougar?'
"'Oh! You're Mister Rose, aren't you!'

I imitate a different voice at this point, a not very pleasant, nor understanding voice, but shallow and defensive.

"'We've been trying to call you for three days. Your phone must be out of order.'

Here is trouble on the horizon and it isn't being spelled out by the narrator--it is being shown, hinted at, through the direct dialogue of a character. Why was the cage door open?   Why has the zoo keeper been trying to call?  Hurry up, and get on with the story!--which is exactly what we want the listener to wish, while he's reaching his own conclusions from the evidence dropped in front of him.

> "It isn't out of order," Al said,"I've been setting up a new ranger station.  I'm at a new phone.  What's happened?
> "'She didn't work out.'
> "What do you mean, 'She didn't work out?'
> "'Well, she wouldn't eat.  She just kept crying in her cage all the time.'
> "What happened?

You see, Al has to wait for an answer too.

(The zoo keeper goes on in a whiney voice now, wanting to put off telling the truth.)

> "'Well, we had the best veterinarians we could get but they couldn't do anything for her.'
> "What happened?

Al is ready to grab the zoo keeper by the throat by this time and shake it out of him.

> "'We found her dead in her cage this morning.'

At this point, I simply let silence reign.   There is no point in saying anything, and a lot of point in keeping quiet.  It's over.

But, after a long pause, I let Al have a last word.

> "The first thing I thought of," Al said, "was how they had told me when I made arrangements to bring Quito to the zoo: 'You need to understand that an animal you've raised in your home,  that's slept in your bedroom, and eaten from the kitchen table, may not make the adjustment to live in an iron cage in an impersonal zoo.'"

After another pause I say:

> That is a true story of a cougar, named Quito.  I found it in a book in a school library, a book called The Audubon Book of True Nature Stories, edited by John K. Terres.

I want the children to know where the story came from, and for them to know where they can get more such stories--the school library.

Those old unwritten rules of storytelling still apply. The first words have to count, and the last words have to count when you come to the end. Everything in-between needs to stick tightly to the subject, which, in this story, is Quito. Wander off and your listeners wander off. Quit before it's ended and they'll kill you. Dribble on after the story is ended and somebody'll get up and knock out his pipe. "'Bout time to drain that coffee pot, wouldn't you say?"

Photo by Mark Billingsly

# Chapter 2

# HOW TO LOVE, LEARN AND RELATE A STORY

I can love a story when...

1. **A story has a character** (person, animal, bird) that I can care about.

    The story comes alive and stays alive

    -When a character takes center stage (a character about whom we feel strong emotion).

    -When the character has a problem to solve.

    -When the character continues to struggle until the last resolution.

2. **A story has a place.**

    -"Next to knowing how to write about people, you should know how to write about a place. People and places are the twin pillars on which most nonfiction is built. Every human event happens somewhere, and the reader (listener) wants to know what that 'somewhere' is like." -William Zinsser, On Writing Well.

3. **A story has a time**--a time of day, a time of year, or a time of political, social or scientific development.

-"It was the best of times and the worst of times..." Charles Dickens, Tale of Two Cities (time of revolution).

-Or, one can be as specific as George Bernard Shaw: "I arrived in Dublin on the evening of the 5th of August..." ("The Miraculous Revenge").

4. **A story has unity.**

The unity holds

-When we stay with the character we introduced with no wasteful distractions or sidetracks.

-When everything supports and forwards the plot.

-When the unifying center of a story is the character in a struggle in a place and time.

5. **A story has sensory awareness.**

A story takes on reality

-When readers or listeners are allowed to see, feel, touch, taste, smell, and hear what is in the story.

-When the teller shows instead of tells. (We can look over the shoulder of the teller to see a baby couger toddling out from Olympia National Forest or see the man leaning on his cane, edging onto a park bench, blowing his nose with trembling hand.)

-When there are smells. Smells often get left out, but smells are some of the earliest memories we have. Smells have the power to bring us recollections of home. Cinnamon rolls baking may bring back with the fragrance the whole awareness of your grandmother's kitchen.

-When there are tastes. Let us taste food in stories. (Tolkien, writing The Lord of the Rings had his little creatures eating at about every third page.)

-When there are reminders of the common experiences of our daily life. Let characters in your stories yawn when they get sleepy (as Tom Thumb does), and stretch when they awaken. In other words, pay attention to the most basic events of our daily life and survival.

6. **A story has metaphors, similes--comparisons and contrasts which help us build mental images.**

One little girl wrote: "When my dog crawls up on my bed during the night, I reach out and touch him. His ears feel like Chinese silk." (Koch is good at teaching such comparisons in Wishes, Lies and Dreams. Jack Best in one of my favorite horse race stories talks about a rider "who was so long-legged he looked like a rattle snake on stilts." See Lon Tinkel, The Cowboy Reader, SMU Press.)

Metaphors can get out of hand. "If this idea ever catches fire, it will snowball across the land." (Quoted from The New Yorker in Roland Bartel, Metaphors and Symbols: Forays into Language. Urbana: National Council of Teachers of English, 1983--which is, by the way, a good discussion.)

One of my teachers at SMU, Albert Outler, referring to an authority, said, "He was as wrong as a bent gun."

And another Texan, Senator Bob Murphy, spoke of the river being "so high you could see under it." I like the picture language which enables the listener to create his own imaginative image, such as the fellow who was so tall and skinny, "if he'd grow'd another foot he'd aforked again." -Murphy.

7. **A story has sharp, clear, pertinent beginnings and endings.**

Shakespeare often foreshadowed the whole play in his first few lines. Conclusions should pick up the threads and tie them in a quick knot and then...STOP. These are the only two parts of a story I memorize: The first line and the last line. The first line gives me the right place to start and gets me into the first scene so I can begin "seeing the pictures." I tell the story from the pictures in my mind. The last line gives me a goal to head for and a definite, well-thought-out stopping place.

Photo by Connie Wirta of <u>Scotts Bluff Star-Herald</u>

# Chapter 3

# TOOLS OF THE STORYTELLER

Sometimes I'm asked, **How did you get started storytelling?**

I think it happened when neighboring farmers came to our kitchen at night and told stories. As a little boy I listened, awestruck, as Art Schultz told about the spring a tornado ripped off the Congregational Church tower and went on down the hill to tear apart Cecil Harmon's barn.

Later, when as a teenager I hitchhiked to the Ozarks and got a job working for "The Walking Editor of the Ozarks," Pete Shiras, in The Baxter Bulletin, I heard his stories. I collected stories of the Baldknobbers and found they made good telling.

**"Where do you find stories?"**

I snoop in libraries whenever I get a chance and interview people on tape. I read stories, then lay them aside, then read them again.

### Some of My Favorite Tools Are Books and Records.

When I found Richard Chase, American Folk Tales and Songs, several of the stories came alive for me right away. The story of the "Big Toe" has become a favorite for children everywhere I go.

I've adapted the story with retelling until it has many places of laughter, but it is still very recognizable as the old story whose roots go back to the Middle Ages.

I like to explain those roots to children. When the priest in the Middle Ages lifted the bread above the altar and said in Latin, "Hoc est corpus," he was saying, "This is the body." To the illiterate congregation, "Hoc est corpus" became "hocus pocus," a magic phrase they could use when they wanted a "miracle."

In later years "pocus" became "bogus" and this word is still used as in the newspaper story: "Police broke up a counterfeiting operation and found many bogus bills."

In still later years "bogus" became "bogie" as in the threat our grandparents used to give: "If you're not good, the bogie man will get you." "Bogie" became "booger" (probably by someone with a Bostonian accent).

So the "booger" in the booger toe story has ancient roots.

Do you see how Chase's book was a tool? The story was not simply repeated rote fashion, but retold and enriched through the telling of the word origin.

Augusta Baker's Storytelling: Art and Technique gave me lists of story sources.

Bruno Bettleheim in The Uses of Enchantment encouraged me to retell the story with my own emotional content. See his chapter on how to tell fairy tales.

B. A. Botkin has a whole series of Treasury books. See the book list at the back of one of them. Botkin studied under Louise Pound, the famous folklorist at the University of Nebraska.

For me Ruth Sawyer's The Way of the Storyteller struck a harmonious note right away. When I heard the phonograph record put out by Caedman (1995 Broadway, New York, N. Y. 10023) with Ruth telling stories and visiting with her daughter about storytelling, I felt, "This is my story teller." Her rhythms, her emphases and her choice of material, all.

Speaking of records, when I heard Joseph Schildkraut read Grimms' Fairy Tales (Caedman), I knew I had heard a kindred soul. I listened to his record over and over until I wore it out.

Now, for you, it may be Claire Bloom or Edward S. Robinson or Richard Burton. You need to find the voice that inspires you.

### Some of My Favorite Books for Stories

Augusta Baker and Ellen Greene, Storytelling: Art and Technique. New York: R. R. Bowker Company, 1977.

William J. Bausch, Storytelling, Imagination and Faith. Mystic, Connecticut: Twenty-third Publications, 1984.

Bruno Bettelheim, The Uses of Enchantment: The Meaning and Importance of Fairy Tales. New York: Knopf, 1976.

B. A. Botkin, A Treasury of American Folklore: Stories, Ballads and Traditions of the People. New York: Crown Publishers, 1944.

Richard Chase, American Folk Tales and Songs. New York: Dover Publications, 1971.

Alfred David and Mary Elizabeth Meek, The Twelve Dancing Princesses and Other Fairy Tales. Bloomington: Indiana University Press, 1974.

Everett Dick, Tales of the Frontier. Lincoln: University of Nebraska Press, 1963.

Margaret Hunt, Translator, The Complete Grimms' Fairy Tales, with introduction by Padriac Colum and commentary by Joseph Campbell. New York: Pantheon Books, 1972. (I first realized that I had never had an opportunity to see but a small sampling of the Grimms' Fairy Tales when I saw the size of this book. It is 865 pages long! Look inside and see what you've missed!)

Max Luthi, Once Upon a Time: On the Nature of Fairy Tales. Bloomington: Indiana University Press, 1976.

Flannery O'Connor, Mystery and Manners: Occasional Prose. New York: Farrar, Straus and Giroux, 1969. See her Complete Works and Letters.

Ruth Sawyer, The Way of the Storyteller. New York: Viking, 1962.

Marie L. Shedlock, The Art of the Story Teller. New York: Dover Publications, Inc., 1951.

John K. Terres, The Audubon Book of True Nature Stories. New York: Thomas Y. Crowell, 1958.

Ernest Thompson Seton (also Ernest Seton Thompson, since his name is printed both ways), Wild Animals I Have Known. New York: Charles Scribners, 1900. See also his Lives of the Hunted, Grizzly, Ernest Thompson Seton's America, Worlds of Ernest Thompson Seton, etc.

Jim Trelease, The Read-Aloud Handbook. New York: Penguin Books. 1983.

And, for an enormous collection of printed stories, stories on tape, and storytellers who will come to visit, get in touch with: National Storytelling Resource Center, P. O. Box 112, Jonesborough, Tennessee 37659  615-753-2171.

Sometimes I'm asked, **"What's your favorite story?"**

This changes from time to time. My favorite for a long time was "The Story of Ghost Cave." Then it was "Quito." Then it was "God Sees the Truth, But Waits," by Leo Tolstoi, and so on.

Sometimes I'm asked, **How do you remember stories**?

I learn the first line and the last line, then "see the scenes" and tell what I see. (More on that in a moment, when talking about charting.)

### How long does it take you to learn a story?

Some take months to learn, and others I learn almost instantly--on one hearing or one reading. I'm sure the difference in time has something to do with my excitement  about the story,  but I don't understand the reasons completely.  Many people can remember a story on one hearing and that is part of the excitement of storytelling in education:  the peculiar quality of storytelling which galvanizes the memory into total effectiveness.

### Do you use any memory methods?

Yes, in several books I have read about the list of phonetic memory hooks (picturable words that have a phonetic component) and have learned them. They're kind of fun to play with and to enable one to remember enormous lists of things.

It works sort of like a card system in the library. If the librarian knows the card number the librarian can find the book that's properly located on the shelf. Once you learn this list of pictures you can hook an item--even an abstraction--to it.

Harry Lorayne in How to Develop a Super Power Memory (New York: Signet, 1957, 1974) presented the idea of using sounds as memory blocks. Here's how I've adapted it to help me remember long lists. It may sound like gibberish until you realize it's a way to build any number of images to help you remember.

You start with ten sounds, one for each number from one to nine and zero. You give yourself larger building blocks by having some alternative sounds that are very similar. The sounds are:

1. t or d
2. n
3. m
4. r
5. l
6. sh, ch or j
7. k, hard c, or hard g
8. v or f
9. b or p
0. s or z

The next step is to picture items for each sound. If the items you choose have real emotional content for you, you'll probably remember them better. The ones I use from Lorayne are:

1. TIE  (t or d sound).

Picture a man's tie. The number one is vertical, like a tie. To remember something, picture it tied to the tie.

2. NOAH (as in Noah's ark), (n sound).

Picture the animals coming in two by two. The letter n has two down strokes. I picture the second item I want to remember carried up the gang-plank, or stacked on the deck of the ark.

3. MA (m sound).

Picture your mother, holding the item, or balancing it on her head, whatever. Also, the letter m has three downstrokes.

4. RYE (r sound).

Picture a loaf of rye bread or a bottle of rye. I see a loaf as big as a bread truck and when sawn open with a giant bread knife, out tumbles the thing to remember.

5. LAW (l sound).

It's hard to picture the abstraction of "law" so picture a policeman, or policewoman, since that person is where law most frequently meets us. Most things to be remembered look funny held by a police person.

6. SHOE (the sh, ch, or j, sound).

What you want to remember is in the shoe.

7.   COW (the k or hard g sound).

Hang it on her horns or put it in the milk bucket.

8.   IVY (the v or f sound).  (Made with the same parts of the mouth.)

Picture a vine with what you want to remember hanging on it.

9.   BEE (the b or p sound).

Picture a bumble bee or honey bee flying along dragging your item, or getting honey all over it, etc.

0.   (s or z sound)

No picture, for 0 is nothing, unless you want to picture a zero.


Now, what do you do with all this?  If you want to remember a list of groceries--oranges, apples, butter, eggs, peanut butter, laundry soap, soda pop--picture for the number one item, a sack of oranges tied to a man's tie, apples spilling over Noah's ark or the animals carrying apples, butter in your mothers grocery sack or balanced on her head because her sack's full, eggs broken over a loaf of bread or coagulating in a bottle of rye whiskey, peanut on a police officers tablet or revolver, laundry soap oozing out of your shoe, soda pop coming out of the cow's milk bag into the milk bucket and so on.

Silly?  Yes, but it works if you make the picture.  No one needs to know how you did it.  You can learn the first nine people you've met at a party by hooking their names and faces to a memory hook.  Then you'll also remember that George Johnson was the sixth person you met.  Knowing the order would be useless trivia perhaps, but under some other circumstances, such as with the learning of the chemical elements, it wouldn't be.

Sometimes you may need to remember more than nine items.  That's when you start using the sounds as building blocks.  Here's how it works:

10. TOES (This uses the t sound from number 1 plus the s sound from zero.)

Picture ten toes.

11.  TOT (t plus t sound).

Use any vowels to fill in between the consonants chosen.


12.  TON (t plus n sound from number two).

I generally picture a ton of gold.  Knox County, Nebraska, has a 12 on the license plate so it's easy to think of Fort Knox.

13.  TUMMY or TOMB (t plus m sound).

Ignore the b in tomb since we don't "sound" it when speaking. Picture Tums for the tummy.

14.  TOUR (t plus r).

Picture a tour bus.

15.  TOOL (t plus l).

Picture any tool.

16.  DISH (d sound substituted for the t in number 1, sh for 6).

17.  TACK (t plus k).

18.  TAFFY, if you like candy, DOVE, if you like birds. (t plus f or v).

Do you see how to build your own system of hooks?

19.  TUB (t plus b).

Picture a bathtub.

20.  NOSE (n for 2 plus s for 0, *i.e.*, zero).

21.  NUT (n for 2 plus t for 1).

22.  NUN (2 plus 2).

23.  GNOME (you don't pronounce the g).

24.  NERO (who fiddled when Rome burned).

"Rome," by the way is 43.  Do you know why?

25.  KNOLL .

Picture something on a little hill.

30.  MOSE, or MOOSE.

40.  ROSE.

50.  LACE.

60. JAWS, or JUICE.

70. CASE (as in a briefcase).

80. FACE or VASE.

90. BUS.

100. DISEASE (d for 1 plus two s's for zeroes).


I once had to learn a twenty-eight page story overnight. I was frantic. I broke the story down into twenty-two scenes, made a symbol for each scene, hooked those symbols on the first twenty-two hooks and presto! I discovered that I could tell the story backward as well as forward. But it really works best to tell a story forward.

And, by the way, if you are interested in learning a lot of numbers, such as telephone numbers, you can make silly words or phrases out of them and then you don't have to carry lists. For example, when I call to get my car repaired I have to call "rocker roar lots" which is 474-4450 (r plus k plus r plus r plus r plus l plus zero). And when I'm sitting in my rocker listening to my sick car running outside the door, it is roaring lots.

However, the best way to remember a story is to pick one you love, see its organization (more about that under "charting"), learn the first and last lines, then tell it from the scenes.

John Chancellor, NBC's TV anchorman, was able to boggle the minds of listeners by remembering enormous numbers of details, said Eliot Wald of the Chicago Sun Times. How did he do it? Part of the secret, as Chancellor explained it, is in a 2-by-3 foot sheet of white cardboard, which to Wald looked like it was filled with indecipherably termite-sized numbers and letters. "I make these up myself," Chancellor says proudly, "and they've saved my life more than once: NJ-16CC-60sub refers to the fact that 16 per cent of New Jersey's population lives in the central cities while 60 per cent reside in the suburbs."

John Chancellor, I believe, was seeing the scenes and simply used a few letters and numbers to bring back those scenes. Wald says, "With a few notes like that, Chancellor could speak five minutes ad lib and yet it sounded as if he had written it a week ago."

I have found another method which is the trusty old 3 X 5 card method of asking yourself a question on one side of a card and putting the answer on the other. Some stories I have all ready to tell except for a few sticky details. Usually those details are names--names of persons, places, buildings, and so on. So, I simply ask on one side of a card, "Who are the characters in 'The 500-Mile Horse Race?'" and put the answers on the back of the card. "What are the rivers and towns?" go on another card. These cards can be held together with a rubber band with the front card listing in big letters the name of the story or group of stories. In a few moments of spare time I can refresh my mind on those key details. I find that the rest of the details come rolling along like freight cars behind an engine. And remember--to use the train metaphor--the engine is the first line of the story and the caboose is the last line. The first gets you started, the last finishes you with a flashy succinct conclusion. More of that in a moment.

**What if you forget part of a story or lose track of where you are in a story because of an interruption?**

If you can't cover your loss, without spoiling the story, simply stop and say what's happened. If your listeners are eager to go on with the story they'll be eager to help tell you where you left off. But, this shouldn't have to happen if you have the scenes well in mind.

**What do you do about the disruptive child?**

Of course, the best solution is to have a story that is so gripping that everyone is completely involved in listening. But, now and then, for one reason or another, a child in a large group may begin to call attention to himself. Usually I simply look at the child while continuing the story. If that doesn't work I stop and wait while looking at the child. This usually has a powerful effect, and does not seem to anger the child.

A CHART FOR STORIES

I found an idea in a quaint old book in the Lincoln City Library, entitled Telling Stories to Livewire Boys. The idea was a chart which I've adapted and used and used and used.

Divide an 8 1/2 by 11 sheet into spaces by drawing lines to make boxes for: 1. Name and source of story, 2. Scenes, 3. Characters, 4. Plot Outline, 5. First line of story, and, 6. Last line.

I find that by the time I have taken a story and broken it down into scenes, written a little description of each character and put down the first and last lines (not necessarily the author's, but the lines that satisfy me)-- by the time I've done all that (and it's hard work) I'm ready to tell the story. The plot outline is helpful for many stories and may even be long enough to spill over on another page.

A sample chart is on the next page.

| Author | Story | Source |
|--------|-------|--------|
| | | |

| Scenes | Characters |
|--------|-----------|
| | |

**Plot Outline**

| First Line | Last Line |
|------------|-----------|
| | |

Photo by Sioux City _Journal_

## Chapter 4

# HOW TO TELL STORIES FROM THE FACE

One little girl told Virginia Opocensky, Lincoln Children's Librarian,   "I like it when you read stories from a book, but I like it even better when you tell stories from the face."

How does a person get from the point of reading to telling?

1. **Find a story which haunts you,** like a song whose melody comes back to sing itself again.

-Does it remind you of something early in your own childhood?

-Does it have somebody in it you like a lot, or hate intensely, or someone you wish you were like?  In other words, does he or she evoke strong emotion in you?

2. **Take time to read the story now and then.** Lay it aside and pick it up again.

        What are your feelings when you pick it up again? Is it the happy anticipation of meeting an old friend or dread at having to read it again?

3. **If certain phrases in the story are "not you," not your way of speaking, then rewrite them.**

        If certain parts of the story are so beautifully written that you think you simply can't bear to tell the story without every silken phrase and jewelled word in place (and you don't have the time to memorize or run the hazard of giving memorized words in a stilted way), then TELL what is so beautifully said to a friend until you find your own beautiful way of saying it.

4. **Try reading a story backward.** (To yourself!)

        Start with the conclusion and ask yourself what led to that conclusion. Go back and see if you passed your own exam, then ask about that scene, "What led to it?" Continue back to the first of the story by THINKING the chain of connections.

        Then, list the scenes on the chart given earlier in this book.

5. Most important, **jump in,** splash! and **swim.** Take the plunge.

        One librarian was so resistant to leaving the book that she didn't start storytelling until her supervisor threatened her job. In three years she had hundreds of people coming to hear her stories. Dare to leave the written page and you'll soon be on your own with you filling in the details.

6. **Put stories into the past tense,** not the "review form" of present tense:

        "He does this and he does that, then he goes..." No! "On April third, 1887, Jacob Mielhausen moved Mary and little Beth into a sod house on Honey Creek..." Make it specific and a statement in past tense.

7. **Learn lists of details for each scene.**

        A good exercise for writers is simply to list the items in a room, or any other scene. Learn items of clothing. When Chaplain Mattingly told me the story of the Ghost of Nebraska Wesleyan, he said, "She wore a long brown satin skirt, high buttoned shoes, shirtwaist with ruffles around the collar and cuffs,. and had her hair bushed up into a bouffant." I had to look up "bouffant" and "shirtwaist" and picture in my own mind how a satin dress would look from the slanting light of a north window. That was a memorable story, partly because of the details Matt put into it.

## 8. Know more about the character than the story tells.

You speak from the overflow. Imagine a person, such as Jacob Mielhausen, image in your mind, until you can see his clothes, the knots of bone under the skin of his hands. Smell the sunburn of his face as the child can who crawls onto his lap at night.

## 9. Know your point of view.

E. M. Forster in Aspects of the Novel says:

To some critics (point of view) is the fundamental device of novel-writing. 'The whole intricate question of method, in the craft of fiction,' says Mr. Percy Lubbock, 'I take to be governed by the question of the point of view--the question of the relation in which the narrator stands to the story.' And in his book The Craft of Fiction examines various points of view with genius and insight. The novelist, he says, can either describe the characters from outside, as an impartial or partial onlooker; or he can assume omniscience and describe them from within; or he can place himself in the position of one of them and affect to be in the dark as to the motives of the rest; or there are certain intermediate attitudes.

Those who follow him will lay a sure foundation for the aesthetics of fiction--a foundation which I cannot for a moment promise. ...for me the "whole intricate question of method" resolves itself not into formulae but into the power of the writer to bounce the reader into accepting what he says.

In other words, the storyteller should know where he/she stands in the story, or outside the story, and in relation to the characters. And the beginners had better be consistent. But what matters at last is whether the storyteller has that wonder-working power to win belief in the story--at least for the moment, and to pull listeners into the story from topknot to toenails.

Photo by Scott H. Stebbins, The Lexington Clipper

# Chapter 5

## PROJECTS TO PRACTICE STORYTELLING

The use of a form to stimulate storytelling started with me when several of us storytellers sat around in a Pizza Hut, or some such place, and worked one of those puzzles on a place mat. The pizza puzzle asked for ingredients of a story. The "Group Composition" which follows was adapted from the place mat. We had many laughs that night and since. It is a way of freeing the group from inhibitions the way brainstorming does.

You may want to copy the next three pages so you can use them as working copies for each project. The first one is a group project. Each person in the group may do the second and third projects alone and then share the results with the group.

## Group Composition

Here is a story a group can do together. Let the storyteller simply fill in the blanks first by asking for a "city," "something in a carnival," "a person in the room," and so on. Once the blanks are filled and adapted for reading, the storyteller can read the composition aloud for the group.

It may seem corny, and is meant to be funny, but it also illustrates how use of details puts life into a story. Here it is:

When school was out, I grabbed my money and flew to _____ (city) to see _____ (something in a carnival) and there ran into _____ (person in the room) and _____ (movie star). They were wearing _____ (kind of clothing) and standing in the _____ (weather). I could see in an instant the weather was making them _____ (The way you feel when your team loses).

I said, "Let's go _____ (strenuous activity) and that will make us feel _____ (The way you feel when your team wins)." Sure enough, we did and we all got _____ (kind of sickness).

That was enough of this so we took our money and went shopping at _____ (famous store). My friend _____ (person in the room) bought a _____ (something with wheels) that was painted the prettiest color of _____ (color). We were all able to get inside of it and go fast. But it made a noise like _____ (kind of noise). When we arrived at the beach our friend _____ (movie star) got us into his _____ (kind of boat) to go on the surf.

By this time we were hungry so we filled up on _____ (a kind of vegetable) and _____ (meat) at the nearest _____ (famous chain restaurant).

After the meal it was time for the show. We saw _____ (famous band) playing _____ (name of song). _____ (person in room) got on stage to help the band by _____ (action done in a gymnasium) with his/her _____ (musical instrument) and using his/her _____ part of body.

This made me so _____ (emotion you feel on a roller coaster) that I left and went home by _____ (way of travel). When I got home my _____ (piece of clothing) was all _____ (something that makes clothes ready for the cleaners) and my _____ (part of body) was all turned into _____ (a kind of ground meat).

I knew that from now on I would do my _____ (kind of work) and always stay in my _____ (a kind of house) regardless of the weather.

## Bringing the Skeleton to Life

Here is a project to illustrate some of the elements of an old classic inversion plot. It is not intended to teach students to write by formula, though many moneymaking writers do that. It is intended as one skeleton upon which one may stretch muscles and skin, and just perhaps it may, with a transfusion of life blood result in the living being of a story.

Have some fun, notice the parts of the story as they go by, see how the plot works. Then try some different ones of your own.

It was exactly _____ (time of day) on the _____ (date). _____ (name of person) stepped out of of _____ (building or place) and noticed it was _____ (kind of weather). The one thing that he/she wanted more than anything was to _____ (something desired) in order to _____ (purpose of desire).

Sometimes it seemed possible, but he/she knew one person stood in the way. That person was _____ (name of enemy). The reason _____ (that enemy person) would never let the desire come true was _____ (purpose of other person).

How could _____ (first person) accomplish his/her goal? How could he/she _____ (say what reaching goal involves) so that _____ (additional good reason for winning)?

As _____ (first person) walked he/she bumped against _____ (object in way) and it caused _____ (kind of pain or anger).

"That was what this _____ (enemy person) is like to stand in the way," he/she said.

Then _____ (first person) got a new idea on how to reach the goal. It would mean going to _____ (place where goal could be reached). _____ (enemy person) would be sure to be there. But _____ (first person) decided to try anyway.

"See if _____ (enemy person) can stop me," he/she said. So _____ (first person) went to _____ (place of goal). There was _____ (enemy person) ready to win. _____ (first person) went ahead _____ (show action). Then _____ (enemy person) moved to try to stop the victory by _____ (show opposing action).

But, in the very act of doing so, _____ (enemy person) fell _____ (or show some other lifethreatening crises from the extreme action).

_____ (first person) saw he/she could save _____ (enemy person) but it would mean giving up _____ (the goal) that he/she wanted so much.

In a split second _____ (first person) went into action! _____ (describe action to save other's life).

Then, to his/her amazement he/she saw that in doing so _____ (goal was accomplished, or didn't matter).

Or: The result was _____ success or failure in saving enemy person. Then _____ (first person) looked at everthing in a new way: _____ (show worthier goal won).

## Using the Senses and Metaphors

Here's one to try to use smell, touch, taste, sound and sight, and to use metaphorical (picture language) comparisons.:

One day Buford stepped out of school. He wrinkled his nose and sniffed. He was sure of it! The dangerous smell of _____. He knew he didn't have much time and he felt his heart _____. He chest felt like _____ (comparison).

Buford went into action. As he ran he heard _____ under his feet. He tears streaked back along his cheeks and felt _____. He stumbled once and fell. When he rolled over he tasted _____. But, he jumped up and ran again. As soon as he got to _____ (person he should tell) his words tumbled out like _____ (a comparison).

Now _____ (the person he told) picked up the phone. The hand on the phone looked _____ (show emotion expressed in hand).

Help was coming. Now Buford felt _____. The rescue people came with the sound of _____ (comparison).

As soon as _____ (everything was done), the people crowded around Buford. "Your quick action saved the day," they shouted. Buford clapped his hands over his ears. He felt _____. He had only done what anyone would do. Now he looked down and saw for the first time what had happened to his knees and clothes when he fell. He had _____ his knees and _____ his clothes. For the first time he felt the pain in his _____. Until now he had not noticed. But he would be all right. His greatest feeling was _____. He had saved _____ from _____. Now people called Buford a _____ (comparison).

(Play with the framework of this plot, try different versions, and see how you can use the tools to write an allyourown story.

Photo by the Milford, NE, <u>Times</u>

# Chapter 6

## MIND TRIPS TO A STORY

Here is a mind trip you can take. Sometimes it is called "Guided Imagery." It is a way you can see again some of the scenes of your childhood. This is important in your own storytelling and writing--to see vividly the persons and places of your childhood.

Charles Dickens once asked several of his fellow novelists whom they had based their characters on and found that every successful novelist he talked to had based characters on persons he or she knew before the age of twelve. Charles Dickens said, "The same is true for me."

Those early characters, scenes, and feelings are the rich ore you must mine in order to tell the most vivid stories.

Here are some directions for a guided imagery trip. You can read them to a class of students, you can have these directions put on tape for you. Have someone with a voice you like read them for recording and then you can play the tape back as you go into relaxation. Use the relaxation session to prepare you mentally for your writing.

## Preparation

Sit comfortably. Feet on the floor. Hands in the lap. (Or, lie comfortably, pillow supporting head.)

Tense up every part of your body for a moment. Make yourself stiff. Tighter, tighter! Like a board! You are totally rigid! Now let it go. Let the muscles relax. Feel every part of your body let go. Feel the weight of your feet, your legs, your hips, your chest. Your arms lie loose as if they weigh twenty pounds apiece. Your head and neck loose--even the skin on your face relaxes and your scalp is loose. Feel so easy all over.

You're on a sandy beach. School is out. Work is over. Nothing there but sun and sky. Just the right temperature. Every part of your body supported by the warm sand. No one around, only a far-off sailboat across the water. You are alone and safe. Supported.

Now you can let your body relax even more. As you count down you will relax even more. Ten, nine, eight, seven. Think of your grandmother's soft bed. Think of yourself at ease and while your body goes heavy, your mind becomes light and alert. Six, five, four. You are doing something important. You are learning how to control your body, to let it rest. Your mind is alert. Three, two. When you get to zero you will be completely relaxed and your mind able to remember anything you want it to. You can take a trip back to any part of your life you want to visit. One. Zero.

## A Trip in the Past

It feels good to be so relaxed and it's good for you. Enjoy the ease and enjoy travelling back now to school days, to one of the happiest days at school. Allow yourself to see your school and your friends. Go back even farther. Walk to your house. See your windows, and the doors. Walk to the door. Open it. You smell something good coming from the kitchen.

There is your mother. She's just pulled something from the oven. She digs into the butter bowl. She wants to know about school. You talk about the day. You enjoy the taste of what she's baked. M-m-m-m. It feels good to be so relaxed and be able to visit anywhere you've been.

Now I want you to walk back through the house. Look at everything. See it again and enjoy. Walk into your room. There is your bed! The same cover. The tree out the window. Box in the closet. Your favorite toy. It's all there. Nothing is lost.

Now you can go from your room to any place you want to go, to any person you want to be with. You're getting there. The more you relax the easier it is. You're coming closer to the favorite person, the favorite place.

Enjoy each other. Walk together. Do something you liked to do. Just enjoy, it's perfectly safe now and you will be able to remember everything when you wake up. You'll have it all. Then you can go to your place of writing and write it down easily. It'll be like writing a letter home. You can see your friends again and the places you were.

Now you'll be coming back to the present time. It's hard to leave, and you can stay if you want to, but if you need to come back, you can come back. You know that you can visit and see and taste more and more each trip. And it will all be useful to your writing. You are coming back and you are bringing some characters with you--people you've loved more than anybody. You will be able to write down about every hair on their heads, about the clothes they wore, the things you ate together, the fun you had with each other. It's all there inside your head, ready to come out when you want it to.

You're coming back now, feeling energetic, power flowing through your body. Stretch and feel the goodness of having had a pleasant nap. Your mind and body are wide awake. You can remember everything you saw and smelled and tasted. You write now and enjoy writing.

**Variations.** Try this one.

Relax. Count down. Do all the steps. Remember someone in your childhood you felt strongly about.

Picture that person in a dangerous situation. What is the danger? It's coming closer. Can someone keep it from happening?

Now picture the person--you, or someone--who can save that person from danger.

Now it's happening! Success! How was it done? You can see that it was a close call. Your story!

**Or this:**

Relax. Count down. Do all the steps. Remember someone you had a crush on. Picture that person again. See that person doing some active sport or work or play. Enjoy watching this wonderful person again.

What would you like to say? What keeps you from saying it? Is there someone else who loves that person too? Here is a triangle. Two of you, maybe more than two of you, want the same person. What are they going to do to get that other person?

Why can't you succeed? What's holding you up?

Why can't they succeed? What stops them?

Now picture an event where it might be settled. The choice made!

How do you prepare? (Buy special clothes? Train for the event? Change an attitude?)

How does he/she prepare? (Clothes? Actions? Things that person says?)

Now the event. Let it happen. Like a dream--you don't know how it's going to come out, but you know you're safe, you're in bed, you'll wake up and it will be all right--you'll have a story.

What choice does your "Crush" make? Or do you make it for him/her? How do you and your rival make up? Any lesson you learned? (Even though you don't add a "moral" to the story, what insight could your reader/listener have? Is there a change in a character?)

Now come back, energize, wake up. Write.

## What if?

Here's another variation on this mind trip.

Relax. Count down. Do all the steps. Enjoy a nap on your grandma's feather tick. You're barely awake and you look down to Grandma's throw rug on the floor.

What if that throw rug had magic in it? What if you could make it lift off the floor? What if it could lift you? Want to take a trip? Any trip? You are safe. You can fly on a magic carpet.

You are very relaxed. Sleepy. You crawl onto the cozy carpet. Amazing! If you pull up on the edge of the carpet the carpet rises off the floor. There you are floating in the room, just above the chairs. You can look over the edge and see down. You are safe.

Tug on the carpet edge. Pull it forward. You sail along, you sail out the door. Pull up--you go up. Pull down--you go down.

This is fun! Higher and higher. You're above your town. You can see all the way to the next town.

You pull hard and you zoom through the air like a jet plane.

You're over a strange land. Go lower. You settle down over strange trees. It's like a tropical forest with a little fairy castle sticking its spires up through the trees.

Pull down until you settle on the path. What a beautiful forest! Trees with red fruit. Trees with yellow fruit. Where is the fairy castle? It must be this way--right down that path.

       "Magic carpet, you stay right there!  I'll be right back in a minute."
The carpet lies still, and waits for you.  Trip down the path.  Around a curve.
Oh, there it is!  Gorgeous white towers like sugar.  Windows like jewels.  Run
to the door.  Peak in.

       A lovely room with a table.  A box on the table.  Wonder what's in
the box?,  It says something on the outside of the box.  "Inside is what you've
always wanted.  It's for you!"  Let's look.  Lift the lid.  Inside
is:_____  It's what you always wanted and its yours.  Take it out.
Hold it.  But you must put it back for now.  You can come back any time you
want.  The box will be here, waiting for you.

       Back up the path.  Around the curve.  Tall trees with beautiful
fruit.  There's the carpet, waiting.  Pull up the edge.  Up you go.  "Carpet,
take me home!"

       You're sailing over your home.  The sun is warm.  Clouds like bis-
cuits.  Settle down, down, past the clouds, past the rooftops, safe at home.

       Now, what was it you saw?  Write it down.  You can go back to that
box any time you want--you can even take others there.

### Inside the Stick (Pencil).

       A college woman told me this one, of how she sat with others around a
big campfire in the woods.  Everyone in the big circle was asked to pick up a
stick.

       Examine it closely.  Find tiny holes in it.  Look it over so well you
could describe every part.  (You can do this with a wooden pencil in a school
room.)

       Now, lay your pencil down.  Close your eyes.  Relax.  You feel easy
and calm.  Nice feeling.  You are getting smaller.  You are shrinking, and it's
all right.  Everything around you is getting bigger.  You are smaller, and
smaller, smaller than a mouse.  Smaller yet, as small as a tiny ant.  There is
the stick looking as big as a log.  You can the see the holes in the stick, big
enough to crawl into!

       Let's try it.  You know it's safe inside the stick.  Nice big tunnel.
The light is shining in.  The walls are big.  Walk along the tunnel.  The light
still comes in behind you.  How beautiful the walls are.  No one has ever seen
the inside of a piece of wood before.  Notice the texture.  Walk farther.
You're deep inside the tunnel and you know its all right.

       Footsteps.  Footsteps coming from the other direction!  You know--you
just know its a friend you like better than anyone.  Sure enough!  "Wow!  Isn't
this something."  You walk together exploring tunnels, looking in strange

rooms. All sorts of things here. Enjoy. You and your friend, enjoy and explore.

Well, it's time to go. You say goodbye to your friend for now. You walk back to the light tunnel entrance. Step out.

Now it's time to grow big again. Bigger. Bigger! The stick is getting smaller. You are your regular size again. Maybe just a tad taller, and stronger.

That was fun!

And do you know, you can go back inside a piece of wood again--any time in your life that you want to, any time you can take a moment to relax, you can get smaller and smaller until you can crawl inside the tunnel. You'll meet your friend and you can talk about anything you want, you can explore any room.

"Would you believe it!" said this college woman, "I have gone back inside that stick many times in my life. Whenever things get tough, I know I can go back and be with my friend."

Photo by the David City, NE, Banner Press

## Chapter 7

# HOW TO GET STORIES
# FROM YOUR GRANDPARENTS

You're lucky if you have grandparents.  My grandparents are dead.
You're lucky if you have parents.  My parents are dead.

How I would love to go back and ask my grandparents some questions!
If only I could have ten minutes with my dad to ask him a few things!  But,
it's too late.

It's not too late for some of you.

Here are some suggestions:

**Take a tape recorder and go to your grandma or grandpa.**

Push the "record" and "play" buttons.  Make sure you know how to do
it before you go bothering them--because they may get bothered having you
fooling around with the machinery in front of them.

Make sure the television is shut off and you are in a room where
nobody else is talking because other talk may mess up your recording.

Tell Grandma or Grandpa that you need this for school. She or he will understand and more likely be willing to help you.

What if your grandma lives in Florida? Make plans to take your tape recorder next time you visit. Thanksgiving or Christmas is a great time to do this because grandparents sometimes get tired of all the hubbub and want to get off to a quiet place.

If your grandparents live so far away that you aren't going to get to see them for a long time, why not write them a letter and say, "Would you please tell me a story in your next letter?"

One grandma in Florida agreed to include one story in each of her weekly letters to her daughter. That daughter, who happens to be a school teacher, told me she now has more than fifty stories from her mom!

What if you don't have a grandparent, or they are too sick to talk? One girl came to school after I had given her an assignment to collect stories and she said: "I didn't have a grandma or grandpa and I didn't know what to do at first. Then I happened to think of a nice old grandpa who goes to our church. I asked him if he would help me with my school assignment. When I asked him to tell me stories for my tape recorder he was so happy he cried. He said that he didn't think anyone would ever ask him about when he was a little boy. I've talked to him several times now and have lots of good stories--some are even stories about Indian days from his grandpa. Now he laughs and says he's going to adopt me as his grandaughter. He's a lot of fun."

When you find someone who is willing to talk to you, both of you need to get comfortable and close to each other so the words will go on the tape clearly.

**Then ask some questions.**

Start with the easy ones first:

Grandpa, did you have a pet dog when you were little? What was his name? Did he ever get in trouble?

Now, by the way, give your grandparent time to answer fully. One time we had a boy bring a tape to school from his great-grandpa. We were very excited about hearing that tape because we knew that old man was almost a hundred years old and had been in a train wreck and remembered stories of the Indian wars.

But the tape recording went like this: "Great-grandpa, did you ever see an Indian?"

"Why sure. It happened in the spring of 1895. I was on a trip with my mother to Pierre, South Dakota. We came around a bend and here came fifty

Indians or more straight at us."

"Great-grandpa, did you ever ride on a train?"

"A what?" (Great-grandpa is still thinking about the Indians--a story he didn't get to finish telling.)

"A train."

"Why yes. We were on the Chicago Northwestern and came to where the tracks were washed out east of Clearwater. Tracks were plumb gone. The engine didn't have time to stop and in it went. We were right behind..."

"Great-grandpa, where did you go to school?"

The tape went on like that and Great-grandpa never did get to tell his stories because he had to go on to the next question.

Here is a secret about interviewing: People will drop little clues about what they would like to talk about. They are giving you hints about hidden stories that they could tell if they thought you were interested.

Sometimes you can simply repeat the phrase with all the excitement you feel and say, "Could you tell me more about that train wreck? That wash-out?" "Wow! Fifty Indians! What was it like? How did you feel?"

When Great-grandpa goes on he's going to give you other clues. Pick up the clues and ask him more.

**Now, you may get so many stories you may wonder what to do with them.**

Simply break out the little plastic squares, or tabs, on the back edge of the cassette (the opposite edge from where the bare tape shows). When those tabs are gone you won't accidentally erase the tape or run over it with something else. The square on the left side of the cassette as you face the visible tape will protect this side of the tape and the other tab will protect the other side. You can still play the tape but you can't record unless you put a piece of cellophane tape over the hole. Or, you can wad paper in the hole. But remember, once your grandparent has spoken, protect that tape. You may never get another chance to hear that voice again.

And, by the way, many grandparents' stories are publishable. The first story from my grandmother that I wrote down and sent in was published in The Prairie Schooner and I was very surprised. I was astonished to think that my grandmother was telling publishable stories!

I believe that many of you have stories in your family that are marketable for publishing. There are two reasons: The things that happened a long time ago are like antiques. They may become more valuable because eye-witness accounts of early-day events are becoming more rare every day. The second reason is that old stories, perhaps told many times or, at least, thought of many times, tend to sift out the unimportant chaff and retain the kernals of grain. The stories may become better as stories not only because they drop out the unessential but also because they develop a kind of rhythm and tellability about them.

This last is what happened to the folk fairy tales. These old stories are worn smooth from handling and are very difficult to reproduce. They have taken on a quality of old oral literature that cannot be created on the spot. Watch for those treasured jewels in the stories of your elders.

**Now, another question arises: What happens if your senior citizen is grumpy and doesn't want you to use a tape recorder?**

I respect that person and can say that I don't like the machine either, not as much as the person. And you may simply need to make notes and then later in a quiet place write out what you remember. It is amazing how well you can do that if you plan to do so soon. I have used this as a technique many times.

One time when my wife, Marilyn, and I visited President Carter's mother she refused to let us use a tape recorder. She had let us use one other times. But this time, "No." She had had a bad experience with a reporter since we had interviewed her a year before.

We listened as well as we could and when we left we drove down the road a way and parked beside the road. We got out a tape recorder and told everything we could remember on the tape. We have also done that with pencil and paper. Simply put down anything that comes to mind--don't worry about the order. Each thing you remember will call up something else and before long it will make connections and you may get an almost total interview back if you can relax enough and let the chain of memory lift out the chunks.

But I do like the easy flow of words that comes with a relaxed interview and the security of knowing later that you are putting down the exact words. (You need to be kind to your friend, though, and not type up the exact mistakes, grunts and stutterings. I once gave back an interview transcription with all the bad grammar and false starts and uh-huhs that were really only incidental to a great conversation. The old gentleman was so horrified to see what he'd said that he never let me interview him again. I learned a painful lesson. So, do be careful and kind.)

I like a tape because it preserves the laughter, the rise and fall of the voice and delicate nuances of words. People communicate so much more than words and, of course, the video camera is making possible a whole new dimension And there is this about our writing that one student put so well: "When Grandma tells her stories they're funny and exciting, but when she writes them down they're pretty and nice--but not so funny or exciting." What happened was that when Grandma took up her pen, she turned on her old grammar school training and became stuffy.

Fortunately, not all people write this way.  Some people are natural letter writers and a side of their personality comes out that you never get to see any other way.  It's as if, when they can relax and take time for their right words to come, they can put humor and fun-filled excitement into a story that they never get to put in talking across the table.  Enjoy and encourage those people.  Write letters to them and draw them out.

But, there is the person who should be taped because he/she has a natural oral talent.  I was called last year about one such person.  the woman on the phone said, "Dr. Ehrlich is 98 years old.  He's been the president of four different colleges.  He has a fantastic memory for detail but he won't let us use a tape recorder.  Can you help?"

I said, "Why would he let me tape record him when he won't let you?"

"Well," she said, "you've interviewed a lot of people."

I went over.  I took my tiny tape recorder which I could have hidden in my pocket.  But that, of course, would be cheating.  I laid it on my lap in full view.

Dr. Ehrlich sat up straight in his rocking chair, a great shock of white hair and a ruddy face.  He was hard of hearing so I had to shout to him.

"Dr. Ehrlich," I said, "I used to live out in your country, near Minden."

We talked a little as I pressed the "record" buttons on my tape recorder.  He saw me.

"What have you got there?" he asked accusingly.

"A tape recorder," I said.

"A what?"

"A tape recorder," I shouted.

"I don't like that," he said.

"I don't either," I said.  "I understand you came from south of Minden."

"Yes, I did."

"If you were born 98 years ago, you must have heard of the Blizzard of '88."

"Heard of it!" he roared, indignantly, "I was in it."  He went on to tell me how his father and mother took measures to rescue their family from freezing.  He told me a murder story of early Franklin County and horse thieves.

At the end of the tape I dreaded turning the tape over because he would see me do it.  Sure enough, he did.

"What are you doing there?"  He pointed a bony finger at the little machine in my lap.  "Have you been recording me?"

"Yes, Dr. Ehrlich," I said, meekly, "I'm recording."

"I don't like that," he thundered.

"I don't either," I said as I pushed the record buttons into place.  "I heard you were president of a college up in Canada."

"I was.  They were broke when I went up there.  The college was about to close.  I told the boys to plant potatoes.  We could eat potatoes next winter and hold college.  We did and we eventually pulled that college out of debt."

He went on and on, telling fascinating stories of his work in Canada and of being president of a school back in Denmark.

At the end of three cassettes I had to go.  While the last cassette was still recording I picked up the machine and said, "Dr. Ehrlich, I want to thank you for a really wonderful time.  I have enjoyed hearing the stories of Minden and Canada and Denmark."

He saw the recorder again.  "Have you been recording this whole thing?"  He pointed at my machine.

"Yes, sir, I have."

"I don't like that."

I reluctantly handed him the cassettes.  "If you don't like it, Dr. Ehrlich, you can have all these cassettes and burn them in the stove."

He frowned.  "Burn 'em?"  He handed back the cassettes and stroked his chin.  "Oh, I don't care what you do with them."

And that got recorded.

So, I had a permission, of sorts, but I didn't feel easy about it.  I went home that night and hoped that I could quickly get the cassettes copied before anything happened to them.  I didn't get to.

The next morning, even before I finished breakfast, the phone rang.  I knew who it was.  I was going to lose the tapes after all.

"Hello?"

"Are you the young man that tape recorded me yesterday?"

"Yes, Dr. Ehrlich, I am."

"Well," he hesitated, "I left out a couple of things yesterday."

Yippee! I was not only going to get to save the tapes but get some more stories.

I went back and got two more tapes full. We got those tapes copied and I personally took a set out to the newspaper at Minden. The colleges got a set, I understand, and so we saved some oral history.

I like that story of Dr. Ehrlich because I succeeded for once. I haven't always been so lucky. Also, it taught me something. Emphasize the person not the machine.

So, those of you who are going to tape your grandparents, learn to know your tape recorder well enough so that you can seem to forget the machine and concentrate on the person.

**Here's another point to remember: Be specific.**

When my mom was over eighty years old I asked her, "Mom, where was I born?"

She said, in mock disgust, "Duane! You know that. You were born at home, on the Park Center Place."

"What I mean, Mom," I said, "is where was I born at home?" It is a different question--a more specific question.

"You were born in the back bedroom."

"I was? I always thought I was born on the kitchen table!"

"No," she said, "you weren't born on the kitchen table. We were going to have breakfast there the next morning."

We laughed. It was good to laugh because we were both kind of tense. Why had I always thought that I was born on the kitchen table? I think it was because I had heard so many doctor stories of surgery on the kitchen table.

"Mom," I said, "which back bedroom?" (We had two.)

"The south one."

"What did you do the day I was born?"

She had to think about that one a little. But most mothers can remember what they did the day their children were born--unless they had ten or twelve children and then they may get a little mixed up.

"Let me think," my mother said, "it was a nice June day. Oh! I know, I washed clothes that day and hung them out on the line. Your father came home from the field about four o'clock in the afternoon and I told him, 'I think today's the day.'"

I didn't realize until later that we didn't have a washing machine until three years after I was born. That meant that my mother had scrubbed clothes on a rub board the day I was born! Maybe that helped bring me on!

Actually, in fairness to the truth, I looked up in the Almanac the day of the week I was born--June 16, 1929--and found that it was Sunday. Knowing my parents' strictness about Sundays I'm sure Mom didn't wash clothes that day and Dad didn't work in the field. Was it the story of my sister's birth? I've told this story many times as an illustration of "how to collect" rather than as serious family history. Now, however, the Almanac has piqued my curiosity, so I'm going to go to my older sister to see if I can get my oral history straightened out. Will she, being a dozen years older, remember what happened the day I was born?

"What time of day was I born?" I asked my mother.

"You came in the evening," Mom said. "We had a terrible thunderstorm south of us that night. I looked out the south window and said, 'They must be having a terrible flood down at Albion.' You came about nine o'clock."

"I did! Wow! I didn't know that. I'm a nine-o'clock kid!" We didn't have a baby book in those days to record all the trivia, and most people didn't. Do you know what time of night, or day, your grandpa was born, for example?

Dr. Graham, who was my friend through my childhood, presided at my birth. Mom talked about him coming.

"A few days later," Mom said, "your father came home from the drug-store in Elgin with some supplies. He said, 'They did have a terrible storm at Albion and a man drowned in the flood.'

"And I told your father, 'A man died and a man was born.'"

Later I learned what those "supplies" were that my father had brought back from the drug store. I would not take my mother's milk and my mother's breasts swelled and became feverish, caked with sour milk. My father bought a breast pump to try to help her and give her relief.

I felt very tender about that. My mother's life and my life contin-ued to be tied together, even after my birth. She almost died because of me and I almost died because I wouldn't eat.

I felt different about myself after those talks with my mother, and that is part of the value in collecting stories from your elders. You will feel different about yourself when you know more of what they struggled and went through.

One time I asked some high school seniors to go home and interview their grandparents, to ask them about birth and death. A senior girl came back to class a few days later and said, "You know what I found out? My mom was born in an elevator!"

The class laughed.

"A grain elevator?" I asked.

"No," she said, "a hospital elevator. Grandma and Grandpa were in a hurry to get to the hospital because they knew they didn't have much time. On the way up the elevator Mama came!

"Every floor they came to, the doors opened and people tried to get on, but Grandpa pushed them back because he didn't want them to see Grandma's body."

No one in that high school class laughed. They all realized that they were getting serious, personal, family history.

Then a senior boy spoke up and said, "I found out my grandpa was born in the cowbarn."

"How did _that_ happen?" I asked.

"Great-grandpa was a real slave driver, I guess. He worked out in the field until dark every night. He expected Great-grandma to have all the cows milked by the time he came in from the field.

"Great-grandma was milking the last cow and she realized the baby was coming. She couldn't get out of the barn so she lay down on a dry place back behind the cows and gave birth to my grandpa. She lay there a long time with the baby pulled up on her stomach and her coat wrapped around. After while she said, 'Well, this isn't getting me back to the house.' So, she got up and carried the baby back to the house with the umbilical cord still attached. Great-grandpa still didn't come so she clamped the cord with a clothespin because she thought she was supposed to. When Great-grandpa came back he got all excited. It was about time! He went and got a doctor and both mother and baby got along fine."

I told this story out in Colorado last summer and an elderly woman came up to me afterward. She said, "I am ninety-three years old. I was born in a sod house and my mother didn't have anybody with her."

"How did that happen?" I asked.

"Papa thought the baby wasn't going to come for another two weeks yet, so he went off to Fort Morgan. Mamma took scissors and thread and every-thing she thought she'd need and tied them up by the bed where she could reach them. My older brother and sister were there, but they were just little toddlers.

"When the baby started to come, Mamma sent my brother and sister to the neighbors three miles away, but they found the neighbors gone. Only their thirteen-year-old girl was there. She came back saying, 'Oh! I know how to take care of them things.' But when she got within earshot of that poor old sod house and heard a baby crying, she turned tail and ran all the way home.

"But, Mamma got along all right. Pioneer women had to put up with a lot."

The pioneers did put up with a lot! And their children who remember those stories are eager to pass them on.

### Make a list of questions.

How do you build a fire without matches? Would you know how to do it today? The pioneers had a piece of steel and flint and a can filled with charred cotton. Striking a spark that landed in the black-charred cotton, or linen, might start a flame.

Did they dry corn? Parch corn? Did they ever jerk meat? One grand-mother told me that her mother used to cut meat in thin slices, soak it in salt and spices, and then dry it. In winter, when the children wanted a treat, Grandma would shave off extremely thin slices of that dried meat and we chil-dren would eat it like candy. It was delicious!

What were the most delicious tastes you remember as a child? What were the best-smelling aromas? We humans have an excellent memory for smells. I remember the smell of my grandmother's house--not just the kitchen--the house. It had a certain smell. Not a bad smell. She was a good scrubber and cleaner. It was just a--well, we called it "an old people's smell." Do you remember that, or something like it? I've had a certain smell trigger a whole rush of memories. The vivid memory of a whole room and the people in it may come back, triggered by the smell of Vick's Vapor Rub or Smith Brothers Cough Drops.

Make a list of questions. Or, if you don't want to do that, buy a book of questions. Don't copy the questions, because they're copyrighted and copying is against the law. Anyway, the people who went to the effort to prepare good questions have a right to earn a fair return on their work. There are several of these books around. One of the best I've seen is called Grand-pa's Story and its companion is called Grandma's Story, put out by the Venture

Management Company, Route 1, Box 73, Morrison, Missouri 65061.   These books organize groups of questions such as "Baby Days" and "The House Where I Grew Up" and "School Days" and "Holidays" and so on.   I've bought these books a hundred at a time and sell them out on my storytelling trips.   The success comes when Grandma or Grandpa actually fills one out.   The books are light-hearted and full of cartoons and spaces to fill out and therefore writing in them doesn't seem so much like "writing in a library book" or something else forbidden.

This summer we told our own granddaughter, Katie, about how I was getting other people to fill out these books, so she wanted us to fill out books for her.   I sat down one day and typed thirty-five pages on the first twenty questions or so.   By Christmas I had a 140-page book to give her and it isn't done yet.   You don't need to say so much--just fill in the blanks over-night--but you may find you want to add extra sheets.

You can prepare your own questions.   A group of children in the Hartman School in Omaha worked as a committee and produced a booklet of ques-tions to xerox and send home to all their grandparents.   Some of the questions you may want to deal with are those great moments of birth, first school days, best friends, driving the team of horses or tractor for the first time, falling in love, life-threatening situations, military service, deaths of family mem-bers and so on.

One time in a classroom at Beaver City, Nebraska, we had a Grandpa-rents' Day.   The children had been collecting stories all week.   Beaver Citians are conscious of collecting oral history because several years ago the high school students went out and interviewed old timers.   They collected oral history all over town and out in the country and published a book!   It's a good book, too, and invaluable to that community.   Those kids who did it are now grown up and several of them are leaders in the community.

By the way, when you invite grandparents in, don't ask them to make a speech or you'll scare them clear out of the country.   Don't embarrass them by asking them after they get there either.   However, I often tell pioneer stories when the grandparents come and I can see them start to grin and remember stories of their own.   I talk about butchering, making sausage, eating spare-ribs, making soap.   I mention mustard plasters some doctors used to use, and Denver Mud the doctor put on flannel around the neck and making onion syrup for colds.   The grandparents start to squirm and its obvious they have some things to say.   It's like watching Grandma watching wrestling on television.   Before long she's wrestling the arms of the couch and throwing the pillow around and you just know she wants to get in there and help the underdog.

When I see grandparents getting into it, I sometimes gently ask an easy question such as, "How many of you ever rode a mule?"   It still amazes me to see so many hands go up, and then come the mule stories.

That day at Beaver City I asked the whole room how many had ever been with a member of their family at the moment of death--that is, actually there and, maybe, holding the person's hand when death came.

Every hand in the back of the room went up--all the grandparents. None of the children lifted a hand except for one little boy. I talked carefully with the grandparents about those tender moments when their grandfolks passed on. They told of Grandma being kept on a cot in the kitchen so Mother could look out for her while she did the housework. They told of coming every morning to take a grandparent's hand. "One morning we came out and Grandma couldn't talk to us. We took her hand and it was cold. We ran to Mamma and Mamma was crying. She drew us to her and we could feel her shaking while she held us tight. At last she dried her eyes on her apron and said, "My mamma went to heaven last night."

Now, that was a beautiful thing, and dignified, for the family to be together at such a precious time. Children were helped to feel that death was a natural thing and part of life.

Then, in the Beaver City classroom I looked out across the children and I saw that the little boy had his hand up again. I asked him if he wanted to tell about the person he was with. He said he would.

He said, "I was home alone with Grandpa. Grandpa got up and said he wasn't feeling very good. He was going to go outside. I watched him out the window and saw that he went behind the barn. He was gone a long time so I thought maybe I'd better go out and see if he'd fallen or something.

"There he was, lying down out in the cow lot! I ran up to him and said, 'Grandpa! Grandpa! Are you all right?'

"He just smiled at me and said, 'Take my hand.'

"And that's the last thing he said. He just stopped breathing. I stayed with him until my folks got home."

That little boy was very proud that he was the one, the only representative of his family to be present when his grandpa died.

What marvellous stories are getting lost every day when they wouldn't need to be. And what boring moments we have had with grandparents because we and they are stuck in the same old soundtracks.

To get a good story often requires asking a fresh question. It was hard for me to ask my mother personal questions, but I got the best stories that way. I asked the old man from Minden if he had "heard of the Blizzard of 1888." Of course he had heard about it! I simply wanted to irritate him into action. If a child asks Great-grandpa if he watched a lot of TV when he was little he is liable to get an explosion of information about what it was like to enternain themselves before these modern idiot boxes were around.

One time I interviewed an elderly couple. We had visited for several weeks and I had gotten hundreds of pages of stories (in fact, over five hundred pages before I was through). I was beginning to feel that the wells of stories were running dry when I got an idea. I dug back into the 1930's history of the little town they lived in. I found a telephone book from 1938 and xeroxed it. With that in hand I casually asked about some names. Again, an outpouring of stories--delightful stories that they had not thought of for years. Mention a name and they could tell you how that person was walking down the street, turning into the grocery store, chasing the cow. They could tell you who his aunt was and the time the boys shot an arrow over the barn and hit their father in the eye, and the time one old hunter sneaked up a quarter of a mile on a stuffed goose that some jokester had propped up at the end of his field.

Even if you aren't trying to collect stories, you can give Grandma a lively time by asking what kind of underwear they used to wear back in the teens. Most grandparents in northern climates who have survived many winters are glad to talk about underwear. One grandma in a Senior Center where I asked the question got so excited she hurried home and came back with some bone buttons from an 1890's union suit. I have one in my pocket as I write this. She told about bringing the "long handles" off the clothes line, frozen into boards that stuck up over her head and then stacking them like kindling wood on the dining room table.

Before my ninety-nine-year-old grandmother died, my visits with her had gotten sort of dry. I wanted to talk about the dance last night and she wanted to talk about the covered wagons. I asked her what her father did for a living back in Indiana and she said, "He was a cooper."

"What's a cooper?" I asked.

"He made barrels."

"What did he do with them?"

"He sold them in Louisville, Kentucky. He didn't sell them empty either."

"What did he put in them?"

"Apple cider."

"Oh. He had an orchard."

"He'd put apples through the cider press and pour the juice in those barrels. He kept the barrels out in that beechwood barn of his, all winter."

Then, a thought occurred to me. My grandmother, who was a strict teetotaler, had just given me a clue about my great-grandfather.

"You mean, he kept that cider all winter. It must have..."

"Oh, my yes. Those barrels would get to bubbling and foaming. You could smell that cider all the way to the house. Lots of times my sister and I went out to the barn and crawled up on top of those barrels with straws. We'd push the straws together if they weren't long enough and reach down into those barrels. I don't know if we got so much cider or if it was just those fumes, but sometimes we'd be sort of tipsy when we came back out of the barn."

Hilarious! To hear my dignified old grandmother telling such a thing about split my sides, but I had to wait until I got out of there.

So we had a good time together instead of us both having a boring time of it, going over the same old things and politely asking such things as, "What did you do in school last week?" (She didn't really want to know, or, at least, didn't want to know the things I thought proper to tell her) or, "Did the cleaning lady get here on Thursday?" (I didn't want to know about the cleaning lady either, but, insultingly, I thought that was the most important thing on her mind.)

Why not ask your grandparents some sexy questions such as how did they fall in love? Did he propose? Did anything funny happen on the honeymoon?

I asked my grandmother about snakes in Indiana and she told how her uncles related tales of hoop snakes that rolled downhill with tail in mouth and killed anything they hit, including trees.

She told about a great uncle of hers who went to the dug well on his Indiana tall-grass prairie and was bit by a rattler. He killed the snake but died, threshing around until the tall grass was beaten down in a large circle.

Questions about animals often evoke an excited answer. Were you ever chased by a bull? Any other animal? Many children had vivid experiences with animals. I was chased by a flock of ganders one time who bit me on my bare legs until they bled.

Another whole range of questions involves sleeping. Did you ever sleep three in a bed? Four in a bed? (One old grandpa said, "Yup, I've slept four in a bed, but you've got to keep your toenails trimmed." The implication is that when sleeping four in the bed the unlucky fourth has to sleep across the foot of the bed. Did you ever sleep in a feather tick? Did you ever strip feathers? Mrs. Exon, the wife of Senator Exon, told me that in her mother's community women used to spend Sunday afternoons cutting the sharp quills out of feathers. Did you ever sleep in the barn? When company came and there weren't enough beds, the men and boys often retired to the haymow.

Did you ever dream that you were falling out of bed? Falling down a cliff? The whole subject of dreams is a rich one for questioning. Dreams of being chased by a monster, of being naked in a public place, of being unable to run, of tumbling down a hole, of flying, of being invisible--these are universal dreams experienced by many people and can be a rich source of stories.

In the next chapter I'll suggest an interview form that you can use, but do consider making up your own questions, or add to my list. See the oral history sources in the back of this book for a wealth of ideas.

Photo by Lori Potter of <u>York</u>, NE, <u>News-Times</u>

# Chapter 8

## INTERVIEW FORMS

Choose a person willing to be interviewed. Record the answers to the questions below. Use a tape recorder if possible, of course, but make notes anyway. This has a couple of advantages. You can have an outline summary without having to listen through the whole tape again. Also, you can note some of the visible and other impressions in the sections near the end of this form.

**INTERVIEW**   Interviewer's Name:_____
**PROJECT**      Person Interviewed:_____
               Is use of name permitted? Yes ____  No ____

1. Sisters? Older___ Younger___ Brothers? Older___ Younger___
   Other relatives living in your home?_____
   _____

2. Place you were born? Hospital_____ Year_____ What room of your
   home?_____ Where was home at the time?_____
   Doctor _____ What cost? _____ Helpers _____

3. Parents work or profession _____

4. What sort of community? (Farm? Town? Suburb? Ethnic? etc.)_____
_____

5. What is your earliest memory? _____

Any smell, touch, taste associated? _____

When was that earliest memory? _____

6. Did you have a pet dog (other animal)? _____ What name? _____
What happened to it? _____

7. Did you ever have nightmares? _____
Dreams of falling? _____ Flying? _____ Other? _____

Walk in your sleep? _____

8. Did you ever hear ghost stories? _____

9. Ever caught in a storm? _____

10. What did you do for fun? _____

11. What was the hardest work? _____

12. What was the most important turning point in your life--a time when you
might have gone a different direction? What happened? _____
_____
_____

13. What events, attitudes, played important part in your life when you were
at a certain age (For example: In the eighth grade our house had burned down
and I was scared of my dad, had to borrow clothes from relateves etc.)
In first grade: _____
Eighth grade _____
High school _____
First work _____
_____

14. From what country did your grandparents come? _____

How has this made a difference for you? (Being Czech, English, etc.) _____
_____

15. Why did your family cometo the state you live in? _____
_____

16. Did your family come by covered wagon? Train? How? _____
_____

17.  What were your father's parents like? _____
Your mother's parents? _____

18.  Are there some stories from your grandparents you'd like to pass on?
_____
_____
_____
_____
_____

19.  What religious ties? _____
_____

20.  Any special family get-togethers?  Traditions? _____
_____

21.  What was your best Fourth of July? _____
Why? _____
Thanksgiving?_____
Other holidays? _____
What happened? _____

22.  Where were you when the news came of _____?
(Ask here of those events that are likely to have happened at an impressionable
age.  I have had good luck with older people asking about the news of Lind-
bergh's flight, of the bombing of Pearl Harbor,  the death of President Roose-
velt, the shooting of President Kennedy, the landing on the moon, of the death
of certain relatives such as a grandparent or parent. This is valuable to the
interviewer because shocking, surprising news often freezes a picture in the
memory of the whole scene at the time.)

23.  Any of your family in the Armed Forces? _____
_____

24.  What politics? _____

25.  What was the biggest "no-no" in your childhood? _____
_____
Did you ever break the rule?  (You don't have to answer that!) _____
_____
_____
How did your parents punish you? _____
_____

26.  How about your career goals?  Where would you like to be ten years from
now? (In the case of retired or elderly, you might ask, What would you still
like to accomplish in your lifetime?  or, What would you like to see mankind
accomplish?  What are your hopes for the future?) _____
_____
_____

27. How do you and your family view America? What's right and wrong? _____
_____
If you could change things, what would you like to change? _____
_____
Here is room to make notes of stories and add future questions:

## Observing During the Interview

There is another aspect of interviewing that is more difficult because we have been trained _not_ to make clinical observations of people. But often some of the most important information is given in body language, in the _way_ the person said it, wore it, sat on it, wanted to leave, stay, etc. I have returned from a 300 mile trip to interview somebody and wondered afterward what color the person's eyes were.

How did the person being interviewed sit? Like he/she was a caged bird wanting to fly away? _____ Rather solid and comfortable?_____ As if it would be nice to get this whole thing over with?____ Did this change after the interview started? More relaxed? _____ More tense? _____
How did you feel? _____ Did you ask something you wished you hadn't? _____ At what point? _____

What color eyes?_____ Did he/she look far away most of the time?_____ At what questions? _____ Or up close? _____ Eyes seem to look through you? _____ Searching for something?_____
What questions or subjects seemed to make the person most enthusiastic?
_____
Any clues of important information you missed? _____
_____ Or didn't dare ask? _____

The hands--large and bony?_____ Small? _____ Veins? _____
Restless, fiddling with buttons or other objects? _____
_____
Wrestling, clenching? _____ Relaxed? _____
Calloused and worn? _____ Smooth, babied? _____
Rings? _____

Shoes, feet, legs--like for walking across a field? _____
_____ Lithe and light for dancing? _____ Toes turn up? ____
Legs crossed? _____ Feet up on footstool? _____

Clothing--for party? _____ For work in office? _____ For heavy physical work? _____ Texture rough? _____ Smooth? _____

Worn easily? _____ Worn like the person would like to change as soon as possible?_____
Names of clothes: Shirt _____ Color _____ Tie _____ Color _____
Coat? _____ Type, color etc._____ Loose? _____
Trousers _____ Shoes _____ Hair _____ Glasses _____
Dress _____ Blouse _____ Coat _____
Lacy? _____ Severe? _____ Casual? _____ Colors? _____

What did the clothes seem to say? I like myself? _____ I'm at ease in my occupation? _____ I want you to take notice? _____ Of what?
_____
_____
_____

Such an inventory may seem too personal, too judgmental for the ordi-nary person interviewing. This is an inventory for the writer. And the writer is not an ordinary person! The writer is a keen observer of human nature, of scenes, of smells-touches-tastes-sights-sounds and, so far as possible, those subliminal impressions the interviewer has received.

If you trust your tape recorder to make notes for you of words spoken, your mind and pencil are set free to record other impressions. Use this inventory for quick checks. Note color of eyes, the way the person's hands looked, clothes (you may have to run, as I have, to some source such as a Sears Roebuck Catalog to get the names of clothes).

Do as much as you can during the interview, but then run over the list after the interview is over and you'll be surprised at how many things you can remember--clocks ticking, the feeling you had about the person's move-ments--hand flutterings, legs crossing, eyes penetrating you or shifting around the room.

What will truly amaze you is how these little details will make your written story of this person come alive. It is what separates the great writer from the superficial one. Making that character become real again on paper after the interview is finished--months later, perhaps--will win for you unbe-lievable rewards.

Voice? Gravelly? _____ Smooth? _____ High? _____ Low? _____ Like a mother soothing a child? _____ Like a comedian who is bursting with humor? _____ Like an authority who can easily give you orders? _____
Like what?_____

What was the room like where that person lives _____ works _____ Tossed and heaped? _____ What did you see tossed around?_____ List other things you remember while the impression is strong:
_____ Orderly--not a paper clip out of place?
_____ What pictures or art objects?
_____ What did it say about the per-son? _____ Artistic? _____ Sentimental? _____ All business?
_____ What business? _____ Golf clubs standing in corner? _____

(list)_____

_____

_____

      Now, a few last sensory impressions: What sounds do you associate with the person: Phones ringing? _____ Clocks ticking? _____ Keys jangling? _____ Dogs barking or other pets? _____ What smells? (even if you didn't smell, what smells would you associate with the room, the person, etc.) Perfume? _____ Aftershave? _____ Sunburn? _____ Spice? _____ Fresh linen out of the dryer? _____ Or off the line? _____ Other _____ What touch would you associate with this person? Soft _____ Rough _____ Scratchy _____ Smooth? _____

      Here write additional notes or draw a sketch of the person, the room, an object that is significant to the person:

Photo by Mark Billingsly

## Chapter 9

# HUTCHINSON LIKES A GOOD STORY
## by
## John Bantama

John Bantama, a reporter for The Capital-Democrat, a weekly newspaper in Orange City, Iowa, asked me some questions after a storytelling session in the Maurice-Orange City Elementary School. He was a most interesting man who appeared to be in his twenties. He was born in The Netherlands, but came to Canada as a small child and then on to Iowa. He went back to work in The Netherlands for a couple of years to reacquaint himself with the language and culture of his people.

In our conversation he demonstrated a keen interest in storytelling and in his story (which I have slightly adapted) he talks about the ideas behind the storyteller's art. I asked him for permission to include his story here.

## HUTCHINSON LIKES A GOOD STORY
by
John Bantama

Stories fill a role in the development of children that would be difficult to achieve in any other way according to Duane Hutchinson, Lincoln, Nebraska.

Hutchinson, 54, a former chaplain at the University of Nebraska for 18 years, learned about storytelling during the 1940's while attending the Berea College Foundation School in Kentucky.

Henrietta Child, known as the Storyteller of Appalachia, was in her 80's when she touched Hutchinson's life. The daughter of a former Harvard University folklorist, she has been an influence ever since.

In the past four years Hutchinson has presented over 750 programs a year. He's also written four books and a dozen articles and short stories.

Hutchinson tells stories and urges others to do the same. He cites statistics that indicate children who are read to by their parents are more likely to go to college. The relationship develops through the way parents handle, respect and love books. "You should read to a child even before he can speak the language."

This is a man who likes to spin a yarn. Stories give children a grasp of their heritage, emotions and imagination, he says.

"The imagination of a child who watches television isn't as fully developed as a child who gets stories presented orally," he said. "Story-telling gives children the building blocks so they can fill in the complete story with their imaginations.

"I feel that important values of storytelling are stimulating imagi-nation and heightening curiosity. It's terribly important to make pictures in your mind. It allows you to go from abstractions to the picture--to an image."

That can't be done when the picture is made for the child. Hutchin-son feels imagination will help them through life.

Hutchinson is fond of citing Bruno Bettelheim, a child psychologist, in describing the benefits of stories.

"Children do have strong emotions (and unspoken fears). If they see someone else in those stories dealing successfully with a problem, they see there is a way out.

"Bettelheim says if you never present a monster to a child, he may think he's the only monster who exists. Children do have violence in their minds.

"A monster is an aberration, something different. A child who is surrounded by sweetness and kindness--soft pillows--feels odd when he does not feel sweet and soft all of the time."

The veteran storyteller likes to share beauty and sadness with his listeners. "A teacher at the University of Nebraska said, 'One of the great privileges we can give a child is to share our own sadness.'"

He compares it to painting. "Dark shadows in a painting get the highlights. The shadows in a story help bring out the bright places."

The stories allow children to laugh. "Count no day lost in which you've heard a child laugh," quotes Hutchinson. "The excitement and laughter does as much for me as the paycheck. Developing a sense of humor is one of the most important things we can do."

Yet another goal of the stories is to pass on heritage. For many generations it was the prevalent means for passing on history. "Stories help overcome cultural amnesia."

But it isn't just history that's important. "A child is richer who knows Rumpelstiltskin. A child who travels to a castle--goes to the ocean in his mind--has more to think about. We want to furnish our children's minds with great thoughts."

For Hutchinson, storytelling all starts with the character. "It has to be a character the audience can care about. The sooner you can introduce that character, the sooner you have the audience with you." Early he also fills in the who, what, when, and where.

He seeks to do these things while presenting the sensory impressions, the smell, touch, sound and feel of the story.

Stories are most acceptable when a character has a problem to solve. "You need to stick with a problem until it is solved, like a good preacher (who doesn't get off the point)."

He says it's a quality many Biblical parables have. "The first line gives you the character and problem. These are universal problems, problems that all families face."

Hutchinson said parents who want to do a better job of telling stories should first look at themselves. The parents' own deep interests should help them in selecting and telling stories. "A personal story from the heart is best. It should be whatever excites you, whatever you believe in."

Once that is done, a person should present a story with a clear beginning and ending. That's true of personal stories as well as ones taken from books.

He says only the greatest actors can memorize a story without its presentation being stiff. "The rest of us tell what we see from inside. The most common mistake is to try to remember the word patterns. You have to have your own word patterns.

"The difference between a bore and an interesting person is that a bore uses a story to tell about himself. We want to allow listeners to see what we see rather than give our own opinions."

He says that means not saying a man is old, but letting the words picture a man using a cane with a trembling hand, taking short steps and plopping into his seat. "You want to show rather than tell."

This allows the child to be part of the character development process. "When I tell a story, we are all co-creators."

Hutchinson doesn't mind telling stories by people like Leo Tolstoi or Nikolai Gogol, writers held in high esteem by adults.

"My own personal crusade is to tell mature stories (great literature) to young people--that doesn't mean stories that deal with adult problems. Kindergartners will listen to a half-hour story if they care about the characters."

He'll even go beyond a half hour and have children stick with him. Any time a story goes longer than a half hour (with small children) he inserts a moment when the children can pretend they're climbing a bean pole, picking cherries from the top of a tree or they can just bounce. "Then they can go back to the story."

An hour's worth of stories doesn't have to be light and weak. "Children don't need pablum, you don't have to make words little. When a child makes the enormous effort to learn to read and then is given anemic material, it is an insult."

When the key word in the line is bewildering, he will present it in a manner that makes the word understandable. "A school child will learn to spell a long word if it is of interest to him."

While many folk fairy tales may not have the largest words, they do deal with large problems. "A child needs in his reading to deal with his life problems."

Traditional folk stories often are concerned with the loss of a mother, loss of food, or sibling quarrels--concerns that worry children. "The story shows a child the way another child dealt with some terrible problem.

"A story must have some kind of successful conclusion. That will tell the child that 'I, too, can solve that problem.'"

Those problems shouldn't be adult concerns.  "We dump too many adult problems on children now.  We try to make them mature too early," he paraphrases from a new book called <u>Children Without Childhood.</u>

One book he recommends is Augusta Baker and Ellen Greene, <u>Storytelling: Art and Technique</u> with a long list of appropriate stories for all ages. He feels the best book on the subject is <u>The Way of the Storyteller,</u> by Ruth Sawyer.

He'd like to see parents tell about their childhood, about family histories and to have children prepare to collect stories at family gatherings. A tape recorder should be loaded and ready to preserve stories on family holidays.

Hutchinson feels it is important to provide places and times for stories that are free from distractions.  That could be during a camping trip or traveling in a car.  "I strongly encourage parents to read to their children."

John Bantama
<u>The Capital-Democrat</u>
Orange City, Iowa

September 9, 1984   Sunday World Herald

# Students' Centennial Task Still Valid 100 Years Later

In 1876, the Third Ward pupils of District 10 in Des Moines made plans to study what life was like at the time of the American Revolution, 100 years earlier.

In searching for written records of that time period, they expressed regret that "we hear nothing of the school children." They wondered if the children of that earlier day whispered and played, and whether they ran away from school if they fell below "the dreadful 80 percent."

The 75 pupils of Miss H. McManema and a smaller class of 51 under the supervision of Miss Sue L. Turner decided to compile a collection of stories, essays and poems that would leave a record of their own school days for future generations.

This collection was reprinted by the Iowa State University Press as a bicentennial project in 1976 in recognition of its historic value.

Today's teachers can find inspiration in this collection for a multitude of projects. Younger children might compile a daily log of classroom activities, handwritten and signed by a different child each day. Another kind of collection might include an autobiography of each child. Older students can do projects that involve researching local history or their own family tree.

## Family Trails

### By Lesta Westmore

Two points to remember in planning such projects are to record them on quality paper and to place at least one copy in a place where it will be available for future reference. The importance of accuracy should be stressed.

Family historians can also include records of school activities in their research. Your personal reminiscences or an oral history of a relative might include memories of the school programs, a favorite subject, or games played at recess. Whatever your particular project might be, you will be leaving a record of value for future generations.

Family Trails is a how-to column intended to assist researchers who are tracing their personal family history. Letters should be sent to Mrs. Westmore at P.O. Box 4244, Omaha, Neb. 68104.

# APPENDIX A

## Choosing Students for a Storytelling Conference

During the four years I was storyteller for the Lincoln Public Schools (co-sponsored by Nebraska Arts Council as an artist-in-the-schools) there was held an annual Storytelling Conference. This was a successful program with more than a hundred children involved each year and many teachers giving voluntarily of their time and energy. The administrative person was Ruth Ann Lyness of the English Office of the Lincoln Public Schools and each year a committee of teachers worked with her.

Here are some notes from the information sheet for the most recent conference:

Here's an opportunity for seven storytellers from your senior high school
--to tell stories and poems to other students who share their interest in this art, and to hear stories from them;
--to hear stories from master storytellers; and
--to participate in a creative dramatics experience presented by Lincoln students.

WHO MAY ATTEND:

Each senior high school may select seven students to attend the Conference. Parents' or guardians' persmission is required (a registration form is attached). Six alternates may also be identified to attend if delegates cannot, etc.

SELECTION

Storytellers have many characteristics, and guidelines for their selection within the school can only be general. However, the seven selected should probably demonstrate some or all of these:
--sensitivity to and positive interaction with peers and adults
--oral language ability
--interest in words, books, and/or use of the library
--ability to tell stories
--commitment to active participation, if chosen by your school to attend. Each student must be prepared to tell at least one story (which may be a personal story) and/or one poem, to one or two other students, and to tell an impromptu story.

Students may be involved in the selection of the storytellers. This will bring storytelling benefits to students who may not participate in the Conference. However, selection may be by principal /teacher choice or any other method designed to minimize student anxiety.

<u>Proposed</u>
<u>Storytelling Conference</u>
<u>Schedule</u>

Saturday morning

8:30 - 9:00  Registration

9:00 - 9:45  Group A, (Elementary) Storytelling by Artist-in-Residence
             Group B, (Secondary) Storytelling in Peer Groups

9:55 - 10:40 Group A, (Elementary) Storytelling in Peer Groups
             Group B, (Secondary)  Storytelling by Artist-in-Residence

10:50 - 11:30  Storytelling Across Levels
               Storytelling, Parents and Storyteller (Artist-in-Residence)

11:35 - 11:45  Closing Activity

Parents and teacher guests are invited to participate.

# APPENDIX B

## Some of My Favorite Books for Storytelling

Sometimes I'm asked, "Where do you find stories?"

I snoop in libraries whenever I get a chance and interview people on tape. I read stories, then lay them aside, then read them again.

Augusta Baker and Ellen Greene, Storytelling: Art and Technique. New York: R. R. Bowker Company, 1977.

Bruno Bettelheim, The Uses of Enchantment: The Meaning and Importance of Fairy Tales. New York: Knopf, 1976.

B. A. Botkin, A Treasury of American Folklore: Stories, Ballads and Traditions of the People. New York: Crown Publishers, 1944.

Richard Chase, American Folk Tales and Songs. New York: Dover Publications, 1971.

Alfred David and Mary Elizabeth Meek, The Twelve Dancing Princesses and Other Fairy Tales. Bloomington: Indiana University Press, 1974.

Everett Dick, Tales of the Frontier. Lincoln: University of Nebraska Press, 1963.

Margaret Hunt, Translator, The Complete Grimms' Fairy Tales, with introduction by Padriac Colum and commentary by Joseph Campbell. New York: Pantheon Books, 1972. 865 pages.

Max Luthi, Once Upon a Time: On the Nature of Fairy Tales. Bloomington: Indiana University Press, 1976.

Flannery O'Connor, Mystery and Manners: Occasional Prose. New York: Farrar, Straus and Giroux, 1969. See also her Complete Works.

John K. Terres, The Audubon Book of True Nature Stories. New York: Thomas Y. Crowell, 1958.

Ernest Thompson Seton (also Ernest Seton Thompson), Wild Animals I Have Known. New York: Charles Scribners, 1900. See also his Lives of the Hunted, Grizzly, Ernest Thompson Seton's America, Worlds of Ernest Thompson Seton, etc.

Jim Trelease, The Read-Aloud Handbook. New York: Penguin Books, 1983.

# APPENDIX C

## Oral History Manuals

Willa K. Baum, Oral History for the Local Historical Society. Revised ed., 1971. American Association for State and Local History (AASLH), 1400 8th Avenue South, Nashville, Tennessee 37203, 1971.

Willa K. Baum, Transcribing and Editing Oral History. Nashville: American Association for State and Local History (AASLH), 1977.

Joseph Cash, The Practice of Oral History. New York: Microfilming Corporation, 1975.

Lois Daniel, How to Write Your Own Life Story, A Step by Step Guide for the Non-Professional Writer. Chicago: Chicago Review Press, 1980.

Cullom Davis, Kathryn Back, and Kay MacLean, Oral History From Tape to Type. Chicago: American Library Association, 1977.

Mary Jo Deering and Barbara Pomeroy, Transcribing Without Tears: A Guide to Transcribing and Editing Oral History Interviews. Washington, D. C.: Oral History Program, George Washington University Library, 1976.

Janice T. Dixon, Preserving Your Past: A Painless Guide to Writing Your Autobiography and Family History. Doubleday, 1977.

Ellen Epstein, Record and Remember: Tracing Your Roots Through Oral History. Sovereign Books, 1979.

George B. Everton, Handy Book for Genealogists. Everton Pub. Inc. 1971

Thomas E. Felt, Researching, Writing and Publishing Local History. AASLH, 1976.

Henry Gilford, Genealogy: How to Find Your Roots. Franklin Watts, 1978.

William G. Hartley, Preparing a Personal History. Primer Pub., 1976.

Suzanne Hilton, Getting There: Frontier Travel Without Power. Westminster Press, 1980.

James Hoopes, Oral History: An Introduction for Students. University of North Carolina Press, 1979.

Allan J. Lichtman, Your Family History: How to Use Oral History, Family Archives and Public Documents to Discover Your Heritage. Random House, 1978.

William W. Moss, An Oral History Primer: For Tape-recording Personal and Family Histories. Primer Pub., 1973.

David Weitzman, My Backyard History Book. Little, 1975.

Traces, A Field Guide to the History On Your Doorstep. Scribner, 1980.

Underfoot, A Guide to Exploring and Preserving America's Past. Scribner 1976.

### Examples of Oral History

Dorothy Gallagher, Hannah's Daughters: Six Generations of an American Family. Crowell, 1976.

Alex Haley, Roots. Doubleday, 1976.

William Montell, Saga of Coe Ridge. University of Tennessee Press, 1970.

Theodore Rosengarten, All Gods Dangers: Life of Nate Shaw. Knopf, 1974.

Studs Terkel, Hard Times: An Oral History of the Great Depression. Pantheon, 1970.

Eliot Wiggington, Editor, The Foxfire Book. Doubleday, 1972.

### Articles

Merlin P. Mitchell, "Tales of Bone Mizell, Folk Character of South Florida." Southern Folklore Quarterly, 35:34-35.

William G. Tyrrell, "Tape-Recording Local History." American Association for State and Local History Technical Leaflet 35, History News, XXI (May 1966)

T. Harry Williams, "Oral History and the Writing of Biography." Selections from the Fifth and Sixth National Colloquia On Oral History. New York: The Oral History Association, Inc. (1972): 1-22.

### Books Using Oral Sources

Barry Broadfoot, Ten Lost Years, 1929-1939: Memories of Canadians Who Survived the Depression. Toronto: Doubleday Canada, 1973.

Gladys-Marie Fry, Night Riders in Black Folk History. Knoxville: The University of Tennessee Press, 1977.

Louise Daniel Hutchinson, The Anacostia Story: 1608-1930. Washington, D. C.: Smithsonian Institution Press, 1977.

Peter Joseph, Good Times: An Oral History of America in the Nineteen Sixties. New York: William Morrow, 1974.

Merle Miller, Plain Speaking: An Oral Biography of Harry S. Truman. New

York:   Berkley/Putnam, 1974.

Studs Terkel, Envelopes of Sound:  Six Practitioners Discuss the Method, Theory
and Practice of Oral History and Oral Testimony.  New York:  Precedent
Publishers, 1975.

Bryan Wooley, We Be Here When the Morning Comes.  Lexington:  University Press
of Kentucky, 1975.

### To Collect Family Stories

Gordon Willman and Bent Hotze, Grandma's Story and Grandpa's Story. 1981.
Venture Management Company, Route 1, Box 73, Morrison, Missouri 65061. (Also
available through Duane Hutchinson, 402-466-4988, or write: Foundation Books,
P. O. Box 29229, Lincoln, NE 68529.)

### Resources for Writers

For writers who are serious, the annual Writer's Market, published by
the Writer's Digest, is a must (gives names and addresses of publishers, a
description of how a manuscript should be prepared, prices paid, etc.) and,
some would say, Literary Market Place (LMP), published annually by Bowker, New
York.  Both give names of publishers, and the latter, more than twice as
expensive as the twenty-dollar Writer's Market, goes into detail about prin-
ters, ghost writers, literary agents, and much more.

Margaret Elwood, Characters Make Your Story.  Boston:  The Writer, Inc., 1942.
Excellent on "how to" of characterization, a classic.

Charles W. Ferguson, Say It With Words.  Lincoln: University of Nebraska Press,
1969.

William Zinsser, On Writing Well.  New York: Harper and Row, 1980.

### Assorted Sources

Amana Colonies, Amana Art and Craft Series II, Amana Artists Guild, Amana, Iowa
52203.

Peter Bartes, Folklife and Fieldwork: A Layman's Introduction to Field
Techniques.  Publications of the American Folklife Center, No. 3,  American
Folklife Center, Library of Congress, Washington, D. C. 20540.

Katherine Mary Briggs, The Fairies in Tradition and Literature.  London: Rout-
ledge and K. Paul, 1967.  Write American Folklife Center.

Finding Community Music Traditions--A Student's Guide to Interviewing.  Office
of Folklife Programs, North Carolina Department of Cultural Resources,

Raleigh, North Carolina 27611.

"Folklore in the Classroom," Indiana Historical Bureau, 140 North Senate, Indianapolis, Indiana 46204.

Halloween: The Folklore and Fantasy of All Hallows. American Folklife Center.

Ralph Linton, Halloween through Twenty Centuries. New York: Schuman, 1950.

Office of Folklife Programs, Smithsonian Institution, Washington, D. C. 20560.

Stephen P. Poyser and Tina Bucuvalas, Introduction to Arkansas Folklore: A Teacher-Student Guide. Arkansas Arts Council, The Heritage Center, Suite 200, 225 East Markham, Little Rock, Arkansas 72201.